Experiences in Community

Experiences in Community

Should Religious Life Survive?

*Gabriel Moran, F.S.C.,
and Maria Harris, C.S.J.*

Herder and Herder

1968
HERDER AND HERDER NEW YORK
232 Madison Avenue, New York, N.Y. 10016

Library of Congress Catalog Card Number: 68–55088
© 1968 by Herder and Herder, Inc.
Manufactured in the United States

Contents

1. Facing the Issue   9
2. Christianity as a Special Vocation   23
3. The Community That Is Celibate   40
4. Religious or Non-Religious   54
5. Revelation and Community   72
6. Sharing in the Lord's Power   89
7. Freedom of Sons and Daughters   106
8. Women of the Church   122
9. Christian Fraternities   135
10. Doing Away with Poverty   153
11. The Senior Religious   169
12. Social and Private Prayer   184
Conclusion   200

Experiences in Community

1. Facing the Issue

The word "experience" in the title of this book has a double function. It is used with reference to the two chief goals of these essays. In the first place we wish to point to a direction for the future. Under this meaning of the word "experience" we wish to affirm that the ideal in the religious congregation must be to provide an experience of human community. Life in celibate communities need be nothing more and must be nothing less than such an experience.

The second meaning of the word "experience" refers to the present situation of the religious congregation. We wish to speak of the experience of men and women now in religious life. In this case we are simply trying to report things as they are. The inevitable result of this work will be to show up the failure to achieve in fact what is usually thought to be the ideal. We will have to examine whether some of the failure might lie in the very conception of the ideal. Perhaps it has always been true, but it is now painfully apparent, that there is a large gap between the religious life as conceived in books and the one that actually exists. These essays may achieve their purpose if they succeed only in encouraging people to trust their own best experience rather than any books which define religious life.

This report on things as they are and things as they might be will appear to many people as harshly critical and unduly negative. Some people who have served faithfully and fruitfully in religious congregations may feel hurt by our criticisms and suggestions. We have no intention of attacking these people or the significance of their work. Their lives need no written defense; they are sufficient testimony of themselves. Nevertheless, if those who have long served with fidelity wish to see their work continued, they must face the fact of rapid and drastic change. One could no doubt make religious houses into homes for the aged but that would be the cruelest destruction of what these people have worked for.

It is even less our intention in this book to write lurid exposé. Little if any good is accomplished by screeching at the top of one's lungs. We believe it to be a pernicious fallacy of our world that to expose all of one's faults in public is of itself curative or even conducive to health. The assumption behind the drive for exposure is the belief that revelation and redemption are co-extensive. There is a basic truth to this belief and yet a terrible pitfall as well. Revelation and redemption are indeed the same process but the process should not be identified with a feverish attempt at sincerity. There is a healing effect in the revealing of oneself, but to reveal is not simply to expose. A man cannot truly and personally reveal himself except within the context of a loving receptivity on the part of another. It is in the personal communion of giving and receiving that men are saved from their own unhealthiness. The communication that reveals and heals demands perspective, balance and reticence.

There is plenty of literature available on all the things wrong in convents. What is needed are some concrete proposals for changing the pattern of life. Although we cannot avoid criticizing the past, our main concern is with what is to be done in the future. We hope that the reader will be less concerned with the biting criticism in the negative part of the work and more attentive to our positive proposals.

The chief obstacle to big change is small change. It is true that social systems cannot be completely transformed in one sweeping change. It is just as fallacious to assume that they can be changed by innumerable tiny steps. There is need for a "quantum leap" that is always difficult to determine but is not to be confused with a moderateness that never upsets anyone. "The real ideologues in this period are those utopian pragmatists who believe that the society can bumble its way through a revolution. They are fanatics of moderation."[1]

Many people who are in charge of renewing or adapting religious life are confident that since things are changing for the better, everything will eventually work out. It may happen, however, that religious congregations are taking one step when it would take two steps just to keep even. One hesitates to be very critical of real progress. Nevertheless, some religious congregations are making a decisive change by stepping out of the sixteenth century into the seventeenth. The change is not only an inadequate one; it worsens the position of the order by making it look ridiculous in its attempts at renewal. If the congregation is going to undergo the trauma of change, then it ought to get to a place that will at least satisfy someone. John L. McKenzie writes that those who think that the evolution of the notion of authority stopped in the first century

[1] Michael Harrington, *Toward A Democratic Left* (New York, 1968), p. 265.

should accept the biblical meaning of authority; those who think that the evolution continued after that time should be with the twentieth century. There seems to be no reason at all to be somewhere in the sixteenth century.[2]

There is sometimes a moment in the life of an individual or an institution when the only way to live is to risk dying. There is no guarantee that a full scale revolution in the life style of brothers and sisters would not mean the end of religious life. We can make no prior assurance about the outcome. This does not mean that the suggestions are vague or general. The proposals are concrete and clear; it is the consequences that are unpredictable. The conservative often sees more clearly than the liberal that one does not make minor changes in tightly structured systems. A small change can destroy a system and it is never entirely clear whether the dissolution of the system means only death or consequent new life.

The subtitle of this book *Should Religious Life Survive?*, is not a rhetorical question. In the immediate future, religious life can undoubtedly survive; very likely it will. The question worth asking is whether it should. For many readers it will not be clear whether our answer is yes or no. Some people will feel that the proposals suggested here are so discontinuous with the past that we are in effect asking for an end to religious life. They may be correct although it should not be forgotten that a similar charge has been voiced at similar junctures all through the church's past. It must be admitted, however, that the suggestions put forward in these pages do not agree with what is in canon law or what is in the Vatican II decree on religious life.

[2] *Authority in the Church* (New York, 1966), p. 18.

Before by-passing the issue of canon law, we would like to say a word in its defense. Although formulations of law should play a minor role in life, they are nevertheless indispensable to any society. If religious life survives as an effective force in the church, it must eventually face questions of legal structure. Anyone who dismisses all legal questions with a cavalier wave of the hand is bringing down consequences upon himself that may be worse than any lawyer's doing. It seems to us, nevertheless, that at the present moment the best thing to be done with canon law is to avoid it as much as possible. This is not as irresponsible as it may sound insofar as many canon lawyers are saying almost the same thing. They admit that the revision needed is so drastic that it amounts to completely redoing the code. They speak of writing a new code in fifteen years, but that depends upon what has come to be in that period. It is the responsibility of the religious orders to create the new life which can later be reflected upon. Through indults where necessary, the religious order probably will have the space to try any new thing it wishes. Some groups may get to the point where they simply cease to be what the church calls a religious order or congregation. If they believe they must do that in order to move ahead, they may be right; but they must also keep in mind that they will still have to deal with the legal question at some later date.

The inadequacy of the conciliar document is a more serious issue. It is of no service to the Council to pretend that all sixteen of its documents are of even quality. They range from the brilliant to the trivial. Although the decree on the religious life cannot be called trivial, neither can it be said to speak realistically to the experience of

American sisters and brothers. It may summarize much of
what was good in the past, but it does little probing of the
future.

For a more balanced appreciation of the Council's work,
however, two comments are in order. First, for an understanding of the Council's contribution to this area, the
major documents are of more importance than the decree
specifically on the subject. Thus the *Constitution on the
Church* (and not only chapters five and six of that document) is of great significance in rethinking religious life.
Second, one should perhaps be grateful that the Council
was positive and encouraging even if it did not lead the
way. In other periods of history, not entirely unlike the
present, the Councils of Fourth Lateran and Trent tried
to pull in the reins on the rapidly changing forms of religious life. If the decree on religious life does not become
a text for exegesis, then Vatican II can be a force for reform rather than an obstacle to further progress.

Councils are both a beginning and an end. At their best,
the pronouncements of a council summarize the theology
of the past and open up a direction for the future. In the
area of religious life, the Council has left the future open
to those who now bear the responsibility of creating something new. To go beyond the Council is not only a right
but a duty. Even were the conciliar document very progressive it would still be inadequate. Those who are fond
of quoting the Council do not seem to grasp the fact that
even in the few years since the Council's closing the situation has changed quite drastically. In America the fire of
new life has been springing out of convents. Non-Catholics,
even more than Catholics, have been amazed by the
change. It remains unclear, however, whether the fire is a

bright glow before extinction or whether it is to be a steady flame. In either case it seems slightly disingenuous to write lovely rhetoric about religious life as if there were not an enormous crisis in progress.

It may be historical short-sightedness to claim that religious life has never had such a crisis before. Emperors, kings and church officials have signed death warrants in almost every century, only to discover that the pronouncements were premature. What seems strikingly different today is that the crisis is so internal. It is not the outsider but the insider who has trouble believing in it. Furthermore, the severest critics are not the disgruntled individuals who could not meet the demands of the life but those who have been generously faithful for years and who suddenly decide that the whole endeavor is not worthwhile. Religious life may survive the present flight and panic but there must be serious questions put to a way of life that does not seem able to stand up to comparisons. People who have wider experience in contemporary life and then come back to religious life may be naïve or misguided, but the fact is that they find it difficult to believe in the religious life. There is, in any case, a dismal future for this life if the exodus of the creative and imaginative does not stop and if there is no attractiveness for the young and dynamic.

At the present time thousands of people who are trying to sustain their responsibilities are suffering unnecessarily under an outdated system. There is no conspiracy on the part of some mysterious "they" to keep a repressive pattern of life. No conspiracy is needed. The simple human mixture of fear, apathy and lack of imagination is more than sufficient to leave us with dehumanizing conditions. In this situation the most responsible thing is not to try to calm the storm but to put forth proposals for action. Structures cannot be redone in a day, even with unlimited amounts of sincerity and good will. But hope must be stirred up immediately. New experiences must be made available and careful reflection must go along with them.

We choose the word "experience" here in preference to the word "experiment." The latter word might be as good as the former except that it has been devalued in the last few years. One Protestant leader recently commented that the church uses experiment as a weasel word. When there is some risk of failure or unpopularity the word experiment is brought in. This move guarantees that the church will never fail; rather, the experiment fails. Unfortunately, this also means that the church has little chance of success in carrying out her mission. The church refrains from committing herself at the vanguard where alone great commitment is needed.

The church is not alone in this desire for improvement through change while taking none of the risks inherent to change. Educational establishments, for example, have long been adept at the game. Yet it would be hard to find any institution that has so misused the word "experiment" as religious congregations in the last few years. "Experiments" are carefully chosen and completely controlled with the express intention of not disturbing the larger institution. If the "experiment" fails then the rebellious ones will have had their chance and been proven wrong. If it succeeds, then the institution may decide to make some limited use of the collected data. At best the results will be innocuous.

It must be admitted again that the conservative senses

what is at stake better than does the progressive. There is no such thing as an experiment to decide on whether to change or not. One can only experiment in the alternatives that are emerging in the change, not in change itself. The progressive, who tries to change an institution by experiments that let the institution decide whether or not to change, is either naïve or dishonest. If he gets what he asks for, it will be an arrangement so defined as not to test the limits of the institution's tolerance. To call such activity "experimentation" borders on the ridiculous. It cannot succeed because nothing is really being tried.

Perhaps religious congregations should put a moratorium on the word "experiment." At least this would put an end to such incredible statements as: No experiments will be allowed until after the general chapter. What a chapter is going to deal with in this situation is not entirely clear, but one can guess. Certainly it will not be with the new experience of church and American life that might point a way to the future. We can do without the rigidly controlled experiments; we cannot do without experience of our contemporary society. It is not scientific conclusions that are lacking, it is a whole broad field of human experience. One will never change the system by trying to prove on the system's own terms that a change should be made. One can bring about change only by convincing people that they should try a different set of experiences that would surely be enriching even if disturbing. When the experience is theirs, the people will change or will have changed themselves.

The question of experience is closely related to that of language. Language might itself be considered as a form of experience or else as an element that springs from experience. Language can be the richest of human forms when it embodies experience and clarifies it. Words can also be obstacles to communication. For example, to teach the catechism to a child is not only useless but is inhibitive to learning. When the words that are not understood are further defined, this simply lifts the words one level further from communication. Words must be born in the interchange of persons; words communicate only insofar as they aid reflection on the person's own experience.

Nothing is more indicative of the absence of life than the stagnation of language. It is frightening to read literature on religious life because it operates within a field of language that seems closed and suffocating. It is the language of those retreat masters who are using the same conference notes which, though marvelously successful twenty years ago, are inexplicably failing today. Nothing is so painful to the ear as a language that has died. However, to recognize that a set of words is beyond salvage does not of itself produce a new and effective language.

We wish that we could promise that all the deadening, cliché-ridden language of religious life books is absent from this one. This is not entirely possible, however, for two reasons. First, we are products of the language that we are trying to correct and no one can fully overcome his past. Second, even were it possible to create a whole new language, it would not be sufficiently rooted in people's experience to be the intended tool. Therefore, we can only begin to change the language, avoiding where possible the worst jargon. Of the rest of the dead phraseology it must be said that one must deal with it and in it, if only to reveal its inadequacy and raise the question of better terms. For example, to cite the most obvious case, "religious life" is surely an inaccurate and lifeless expression, a point which we shall develop in chapter four. Occasionally, we shall use other descriptive phrases for the reality we are speaking of. For the moment, however, "religious life" is unavoidable for securing some continuity and avoiding contortions of language.

The last word of this introduction is an introductory word on community. This is a word which has suffered at the hands of religious congregations, though the history is not all bad on this score. Furthermore, community is a key issue throughout civil as well as church society. It is of such importance that the word is worth fighting for. If community is dead, then there is little hope for anybody. The word "community" is probably not dead, but there is little doubt that the word is often misplaced. More precisely, there is seldom awareness of the ambiguity of meaning or the variety of levels for the word "community."

One hears people in religious life today speak of "building community." Many of them presumably understand the task they are engaged in. Their language, nevertheless, could give the impression that they are concerned with an external construction job. Worse, however, would be the assumption that there is only one meaning for the word "community" and that community must be identified with the characteristics which the liberal-minded religious associates with it. If one were to make such an assumption he would underestimate the profound meaning of the word "community" while at the same time he would overestimate the one expression of community he recognizes.

It is important that we set forth in the following pages a solid basis for the word "community." Once this is done it will be evident that the task of human beings is not so much to create community as to recognize it. Christian belief implies that the community is mankind and it is waiting to be accepted. Saying that community does not have to be "built" does not do away with the function of groups such as religious sisters and brothers. It becomes more imperative than ever that people express a variety of human communities for the sake of the human community. To be an operative and effective community that points to the unity of mankind is no easy task. For religious congregations there will be required conditions and attitudes more demanding than have usually been assumed.

The failure to understand the issue is reflected in two misuses of the word "community." Many congregations of sisters use the word "community" to refer to the whole congregation as well as to the local group. They may never stop to realize that the difference between these two is not one of size. In the sense of an operative, supporting group, the congregation cannot possibly function as a community. On the other hand, as the ideal to be recognized and realized it is narrow and pretentious to call one's religious congregation "the community." At best the congregation is a good human organization that is held together by common goals or ideals. Using the word community for a religious congregation obscures both the present need and the future ideal.

The other very dubious use of the word community is its identification in church documents with "common life." That a community of people will do some things together is no doubt true; but to equate community with doing all things in common is appallingly unimaginative. It presumes that a human unity is achieved by getting conformity to a pre-established pattern. We will claim in these essays that this kind of conformity is almost the exact opposite of a human community. Besides misconstruing the basis on which communities exist, the "common life" assumption would also exclude many other forms of community that are growing up in the world. Religious congregations have thought of the local group as the one form of community. Locality does remain one of the main principles for the expression of community. It may be the usual foundation, but who can say that it is a necessary one? One can conceive of people who meet for a few intensive hours each week and who form a more effective human unity than most people who live under one roof. The world is not composed of geographical units and daily schedules; it is made up of people, many of whom live in various places, function in several roles and draw their human support from a wide range of companions. The religious congregation, one would suppose, would be an excellent place to try realizing communities other than on a local basis.

The claim put forward in this book is that religious life ought to be an experience of community. Some people will find this to be too modest a claim, though they probably do not grasp that it is less modest than it appears to be. Many people will think that if religious life cannot claim to be more than this, then it will not be compellingly attractive to potential members. They may be right, but we do not see any other route worth traveling. We certainly have no heart for propaganda. The people who are in religious congregations will convince by their lives or else religious life will not be bought no matter what arguments are brought forth.

Perhaps religious life is a much greater thing than we make it to be in these pages. If so, we have preferred to err in this direction rather than in the opposite one. Religious life, it would seem, has suffered from the pretentiousness of claims made about it. Like the government's war on poverty, it may not be bad, but it suffers by not living up to the exaggerated promises made beforehand. The greatest sin that the present world recognizes is insincerity, and on this point religious life is particularly vulnerable. The charge made against religious is that they say one thing and do another. If they do not live by the inflated rhetoric, why do they not drop it? Can they not say what they are about and get on with doing it? Any final judgments can be left to someone else.

2. Christianity as a Special Vocation

Vocation directors in religious congregations have nearly done away with the advertisements which imply that everyone has a vocation to religious life, though only a minority are generous enough to accept it. This approach may never have been widespread in its most blatant form, but it can hardly be denied that there has been an element of it pervading literature on religious life. Before the advance of a vocal lay movement there has been a gradual retreat from this position. It may be asked, however, whether the position has been abandoned joyfully or grudgingly, and more basically, whether the terrain has been surrendered but with no real change of outlook.

The point to be raised here at the beginning is that the real revolution in thinking is not in the theology of religious life but in the theology of church. The real question pertains not to the unusual choice to be a religious but to the unusual vocation to be a Christian. Literature on religious life almost invariably begins with the narrow framework of vocation within the church. It is considered very liberal to say that the word "vocation" extends to every Christian. It is thought that there are a variety of vocations in the church and no one is called to be an imperfect Christian. It is always assumed without question that it is a good thing for each man to be a Christian and that every man can and should be a Christian.

Much writing on religious life appears to have a strong

ecclesiological base, but in fact it fails to grasp what is the most crucial question about the church, namely, the relation to non-church. Just as a "state of life" can be understood only in relation to other states, so, too, the consciousness of the church shifts radically when it looks outward to the world beyond church. The issue of church, therefore, can be treated as a series of intramural niceties or else it can be a raising of the most fundamental question of existence. The consideration of the church in this latter context will not do away with all intramural questions, but it may considerably transform some of them. In recent years, the failure to deal with the basic ecclesiological question has had a vitiating effect upon considerations of religious life. Consciously or unconsciously, religious congregations model themselves upon their idea of the church's place and function in the world. If contemporary ecclesiology has not been brought to bear upon the matter, then one can be sure that no real revolution has occurred in thinking on religious life.

It is not so many years ago that the church was regarded as a society set apart from temporal society. The church was an ark of salvation in the midst of a sinful world. Or, the church might have been described as a big place with all the doors shut. Since salvation was within the church, the important thing was to get as many people as possible inside the walls and to keep all the doors closed.

It is easy enough to point out the inadequacies of this ecclesiology; it would be possible to make fun of it. But it may be remarked that these long-held notions were not entirely wrong. Even more to the point is the fact that he who abandons them must come up with something better. It may be right to say that the doors should be opened and people should be invited to leave. Such an invitation implies, however, that the one inviting has some reason to stay. It would seem incumbent on him to try to explain what value there is in belonging to the church.

Until recently it seemed evident to Catholics why they were members of their church. It was here that divine truth, divine grace and divine salvation were to be found. For many people this is still their reason for belonging. The fact is, however, that the changes in theological circles have gradually eroded the position to the extent that a whole new foundation is needed. In an earlier era, men could say "outside the church there is no salvation"; this was a clear statement on the need for membership. Over the centuries the formula was reinterpreted, watered down and finally made innocuous. One can now put the formula to rest, but that will not constitute a solution. One could conceivably make the formula into a redefinition of the church, namely, wherever there is salvation there is church. However, problems of this kind cannot be solved by a verbal twist. There may be legitimacy in extending the word "church" to the whole world, but that would leave unresolved this meaning of the word in relation to the visible, social reality that still exists in history.

The question we are raising is not a theoretical puzzle for the preoccupation of theologians. Many people have staked their life's work and their very lives on the truth of the church's teaching, the value of her sacraments and the validity of her way of life. They do not take kindly to a rather blasé attitude on the part of theologians facing the question. No one is suffering more from this rethinking of church than the foreign missioner who has spent his life in the heroic task of "converting souls to Christ." To be told that this was all unnecessary and probably even bad is dismaying to say the least.

The sad and ironic thing is that it is the missioner who has largely been responsible for the theologians' rethinking. The missioner finds himself caught at this moment half way in a revolution. He has begun a process which will eventually lead to thinking of missionary work not as a peripheral function of the church but as the very essence of the church. Unfortunately, he may have been working in the jungle for the past fifteen years instead of following the theological debates. Since he now finds himself at a loss to follow the exegetical and theological intricacies, he wonders whether he has any place at all in the church. At the very moment when missionary work is about to re-emerge in a more exalted place than it ever had in the old church, the individual missioner may be thinking of himself as useless. He is subject to a cruel trick of living in the interim between the point at which he began the renewal and the time at which he will gain its benefits. If he can hold on until the theologians finish their recasting of old thought patterns, he will find himself at the tip of the arrowhead. Yet it is doubtful how long men can be told to hang on when they have little visible support.

What is most obviously the case with the foreign missioner is to some extent true of every Christian engaged in pastoral work. This would include people in religious congregations. The witnessing to the gospel by works of service and the expressing of Christianity by a variety of life styles have not become outdated. It is more likely that for the first time in history they are coming fully into their own. Yet at this precise moment, none of the church's works is secure beyond question; and nowhere in the church is there a greater malaise than in the religious congregations. One can only hope that what is worth saving here will survive. If anything is certain, it is that this survival will not be achieved by clinging to an outdated notion of the church. To find the new meaning of church one must let go of the old. The two are not completely contradictory; the old will to a large extent be subsumed in the new. Nevertheless, it is just as with reason and faith: they are not opposed, but there is a moment when one must let go of the former to reach the latter. Faith, said Kierkegaard, is like floating on 70,000 fathoms; but you cannot do that so long as you keep one foot on the bottom of the lake.

Not to let go of the past and not to go where faith leads us would seem to indicate a lack of trust in God. Of course, it must be candidly admitted that there is a real risk here. Particular organizations may find that it is too late for reform and that they have passed the point of no return. But they might at the very least find a better way to die. We cannot pretend to be the experts worth trusting for the renewal of religious life. We can only claim to point out that, if one is going to trust at all, it would best be in God and in the human beings who are willing to use their intelligence and freedom.

The mysterious and peculiar vocation that must be discussed, therefore, is not religious life but Christianity. The paradox of the Christian position is pointed to in this statement of Paul Tillich's: "It is the greatness of Christianity that it can see how small it is. The importance of being a Christian is that we can stand the insight that it is of no importance . . . It is the maturest fruit of Christian understanding to understand that Christianity, as such, is of no avail."[1] Tillich is not engaging here in word play or in pious sentiments; he is dealing with the heart of the biblical tradition. It is the central theme of the prophets that some men are "chosen" and yet the choice has nothing to do with human merit. To be chosen means that one is put in the precarious position of being mis- understood as better than other men, whereas the choice is meant only to confront all men with their own destinies.

"The prophets of Israel have never announced a God upon whom their hearers' striving for security reckoned. They have always aimed to shatter all security and to proclaim in the opened abyss of the final insecurity the unwished-for God who demands that his human creatures become real, become human, and confounds all who im- agine that they can take refuge in the certainty that the temple of God is in their midst."[2]

In the last sentence we strike upon the universal voca- tion of man, namely, to be man. "I am born a man," writes Rabbi Heschel, "and now my task is to become human." For many Catholics schooled in the ways of supernatural life, these statements probably sound like the abandon- ment not only of Christianity but of any religious faith. We admit that there is a danger that this trend could be so misunderstood. Nonetheless, the danger must not keep us from trying to reground the meaning of church in a fully ecumenical stance. The Christian is one who must see that God is not a Christian but the creator of the world, that he does not call to perfection a church but the universe groaning in travail.

Faced by the billions of non-Christians who are also

[1] *The New Being* (New York, 1955), p. 19.
[2] Martin Buber, *Eclipse of God* (New York, 1957), p. 73.

God's children, the Christian has been forced to reassess his conception of Christianity. This reconsideration leads to the notion of church not as the place of salvation but as a light of revelation. It is not that Christianity claims to possess something; only that it claims to point to someone. This is still a large claim, of course; and when made only verbally a most unconvincing one. But where a Christ-like life is demonstrated by living communities, there might still be a word for our world.

The church, insofar as she is true to her own nature, must be primarily composed of free, adult, dedicated communities. Where this kind of reality does not exist, then the inevitable tendency is to construct a system of impersonal objects and to maintain it by proselytizing and propaganda. "Propaganda's essential character is a lack of expectant hope and an absence of due humility. The propagandist has to impose himself. He has to resort to himself, to his word (verbosity being a characteristic of every propagandist). In short, the propagandist tries to make exact copies of himself."[3] There may be feverish activity to bring converts into the system of perfect replicas. The motivation, unfortunately, may be one that springs largely from fear and the attempt to escape personal responsibility. It is the attitude that Eric Hoffer brilliantly described in his little classic, *The True Believer.*[4]

The contrasting picture would be of a church that has enough courage to show herself to the world as she is. It would be a church that is not upset by the fact that some people do not accept the same truth she does. This kind of

[3] Johannes C. Hoekendijk, *The Church Inside Out* (Philadelphia, 1966), p. 23.
[4] New York, 1951.

church is confident of her own worth and does not have to make screeching arguments in her own defense. Such a church can be truly tolerant of other men's beliefs not in spite of but because of her own strong convictions. The church can respect other beliefs because she understands what it is to have belief. Asserting one's own truth is not only compatible with tolerance for others, it is an indispensable aid.

This last point needs careful attention. Giving up all of one's convictions is not the way to be tolerant or ecumenical. Many people who pride themselves on being the most radical thinkers in the church seem to have done an about face; they love every church but their own. One must be suspicious of such reversals. It is a well documented fact that legalism and licentiousness, though on the surface opposites, spring from the same mentality. Likewise, the most dogmatic people become the most anti-dogmatic people with the result that they can be very dogmatic about their anti-dogmatism. The same people who used to claim that Christianity had all the answers are now the ones saying that it has no answers. The erstwhile triumphalist now scourges the church for her inhumanity, but there may have been little real change in the mentality of the critic. He would deny it heatedly, but he still is working on triumphalist principles. Only now he finds the church indefensible on those terms.

What is needed is a calm perception of the church of the present and the church of the past, the church of greatness and the church of corruption. In this perspective the church will be found to have many partial answers because she makes claim to no complete answers. The church will go out to others neither to subject them nor to be subjected to them but to share the richness which she indeed has. The church will make many mistakes and have to be corrected but it will be because she has taken a forthright stand on concrete issues rather than mouthing generalities in safe abstraction.

Faced with this puzzling, complex church, the individual must decide whether he thinks the values are worth struggling for. He must ask himself whether he can live with the paradox of Christianity's pointing to the greatest while often ending up the least. Speaking of Christianity's effect upon the West, Arend Th. van Leeuwen has written: "This civilization has engendered not only the most bizarre forms of race prejudice, religious narcissism, social self-idolization and ultra-primitive narrow-mindedness, but also a universal outlook, a sustained and revolutionary self-criticism, a compulsive quest for radical renewal, an indefatigable thirst for discovery and adventure and that marvelous passion for 'objective' knowledge, which is the motive power of modern science and also impels cultural anthropology to break through every barrier of pride and prejudice and provincial isolation which Western man has erected against other cultures."[5]

There is no humility in denying what one has to give. Error is not eradicated by denying that one has any truth. Christianity offers something very good even if it is mixed with the bad. The church believes in what it has to offer, though not without self-criticism. The Christian's role, particularly today, is to be a "no" to the absolute character of any humanism. Such a role can be accomplished, however, only with the concrete affirmation of a particular

[5] *Christianity in World History* (New York, 1966), p. 34.

humanism. Christianity accepts its own humanism as one always questionable and ready for revision.[6]

In this light the role of the missioner (and every Christian) comes back into focus. He goes with the mandate to preach the gospel to all peoples but not with the expectation that all will be baptized (see Mt. 28:18). He *goes* because he has something very valuable that he thinks is worth sharing with others. *He* goes because what is offered is inseparable from the person of the Christian. There is no pretentiousness in these beliefs. If Christianity has something to give it also has much to receive. It cannot fully be itself until it has encountered all people. To say that the missioner does not now aim at the immediate conversion of the individual is not the last word. One need not deny that the missioner can work and hope for the acceptance of the gospel by a community. If the missioner did not believe that it was good for someone to accept his message, he would not be there.

The assimilation of the gospel over a period of time not directly controllable by the church will keep authentic both the Christian gospel and the life of the community accepting it. Christianity will not be turned into a weird hybrid for the sake of lengthy baptismal rolls. Likewise, the positive elements in other religions will be preserved and cultivated. The Christian can wait patiently because it is his own Christian faith that leads him to see that non-Christianity is the usual, ordinary and most common way of salvation. "If the non-Christian religions therefore are proper ways of salvation, God's epiphany in special sacred history is much more luminous than ever it could

[6] Karl Rahner, "Christian Humanism," *Journal of Ecumenical Studies,* IV (Summer, 1967), pp. 375 f.

be if it were in contrast to religions that were to be judged entirely negatively. Depreciation of non-Christian religions in no way contributes to make the dignity of Christian belief stand out more clearly. Precisely the contrary is the case."[7] It is only the insecure who think that they must become more by making everyone else less.

From this consideration it should emerge that there is no need to water down the Christian claim to uniqueness. There is no denial of belief in Jesus Christ as the definitive, unsurpassable manifestation of God with us. This belief may sound arrogant but it certainly is not narrow, for it claims to be expressing what is present in every human life. The uniqueness of Christ and the uniqueness that the Christian seeks is not the dominating power of exclusivity but the receptive center of inclusivity. One can try to be different either by controlling others (with the result that one is not different because the others are all reduced to the same level); or else by being open to all (with the result that one is unique because the others become themselves). There is plenty of uniqueness in being a "zone of truth" and there is an obvious need for such a sign; the only question is whether Christians are up to the task.

Karl Rahner has made famous the notion of anonymous or latent Christianity. He has himself admitted that these are not adequate terms and that they are likely to be misunderstood outside of their context.[8] Nevertheless, it would be more inadequate simply to dismiss the terms as mean-

[7] Heinz Schlette, *Towards a Theology of Religions* (New York, 1966), p. 94.

[8] "Atheism and Implicit Christianity," *Theology Digest,* Sesquicentennial Issue (February, 1968), p. 43.

ingless. One can say that Jesus Christ is the exclusive way of God to man and that all other attempts are human idols (as the early Barth seemed to say). One can reduce all religions into syncretism or indifferentism (as the liberalism Barth opposed seemed to do). But if one wishes to maintain *both* belief in the uniqueness of Christ *and* the necessity of a completely ecumenical stance, then one needs a theological link. Ineluctably, one is led to the claim that all men are already related to Christ. The church, in such a theology, is the making visible what is present everywhere. The Christians, for all their claims, are saved from any boast of superiority. "They only confess—we were blind in our distrust of being, now we begin to see; we were alien and alienated in a strange, empty world, now we begin sometimes to feel at home; we were in love with ourselves and all our little cities, now we are falling in love, we think, with being itself, with the city of God, the universal community of which God is the source and governor."[9]

The use of the phrase "anonymous Christian," therefore, is meant to affirm, among other things, that the human race has one destiny. The bond here affirmed which unites all men will lead the Christian to say to the non-Christian: Above all else, become what you are. In the circumstances of the present this policy would in all likelihood lead to fewer people being church members. But that will probably occur in any case, so that it might be better to open the doors and invite people to leave if they wish. At least people could be encouraged to inquire of themselves whether they might be more free outside the

[9] H. Richard Niebuhr, *The Responsible Self* (New York, 1963), pp. 177 f.

church. If it were preached quite candidly that salvation is also to be found outside church membership, there might be an increase of freedom for everyone. These statements may sound harsh and judgmental, but they are not so at all within the matrix of ideas presupposed. It is not the business of individuals, including church officials, to decide who is in God's favor. The only issue here is that individuals ought to be allowed to accept Christian membership with freedom or to leave without a guilty conscience.

It is not that Christianity should be uninterested in numbers. A Christian is one who is concerned with the biggest possible number, namely, everybody. But precisely because Christianity demands a concern with the whole world, it will probably be accepted by only a few people. Christ did not say: Go out and bring in as many people as possible. He said: Go out and preach the gospel to every nation on earth. Our spreading everything a little thinner and keeping all the doors closed will not enable us to reach everybody in the universe. Perhaps the church would do better in having a few people who were really interested and whose faith might be aroused. They would be concerned not with the Catholic church in America but with all the peoples of the earth.

The church is not one society running parallel to other groups, with each having a particular and exclusive end. The church exists to support the human endeavor to be human and to remind men that there may be more to the human than what they can see. This is not a vague or general purpose; it is a very clear although not an exclusive one. Writers have stopped identifying the religious life as the only way of "acquiring perfection." However, there would still be a narrowness of vision if the call to perfection were attributed merely to all Christians. It is the task of mankind to perfect mankind. People who want a more specific or more particular goal for Christianity do not seem to appreciate either the arduousness of the task or the importance of the outcome that the human race should become human. Emmanuel Mounier once wrote: "Nothing more can be asked of the Christian of today who pretends to become an angel by fleeing man and cursing him, than that he become a man, fully a man; that he have such a passion for every man without exception, that it can be said of him that he made himself a man, fully a man."[10]

If this is true of the church and the Christian, it is obviously true of religious life and individual congregations. One ought not to begin by defining the specific goals. Here is the best example of a society in which the persons should precede the goals.[11] The specific work of the congregation may never be more than hazily defined. This does not mean that the people in it do not know what they are about. Most people are not very adept at defining what it means to be human, but they recognize some things that seem to contribute to the human and other things which are certainly opposed to it. Religious congregations need not prove they have some distinctiveness, nor should they prematurely justify their works on the basis of the gospel. The most successful work will probably be accomplished by the members getting on with something that men can recognize as worthwhile. Presumably a congregation will

[10] Quoted in Constantin Amarin, *The Church in the Service of Liberty* (St. Louis, 1963), p. 29.

[11] See Bernard Besret, "The Problem of the Ends of Religious Life," in *Religious Orders in the Modern World,* ed. Gerard Huyghe (Westminster, 1966), p. 28.

have some very broad category (for example, education) that is the umbrella for its different operations. It is difficult to say how general this purpose could be while maintaining some unity, but the greater the diversity within unity the richer will be the lives of the members. The specific tasks of the congregation may be and probably should be constantly changing.[12]

It is sometimes said that a religious congregation has no purpose for existence if what it is doing could be done by concerned Christian laymen. If anything, this is an argument in support of the congregation's existence. That the work might be done by concerned Christan laity is a good sign; that the work might be done by concerned secular humanists may be even better. The relevant questions are: 1) whether the work is worth doing; 2) whether it is being done by someone else. As a work is handled more and more by others, the religious group should think of other specific jobs. It presumably should look for those jobs that are most urgent, have the most risk and require the greatest staying power. Anyone who thinks that there are no longer any such tasks has not looked much at the American landscape. If people in religious congregations keep getting phased out of their jobs, they should after a moment of rejoicing move on to new ones. The point we wish to stress here is that religious congregations will never justify their existence by finding some task that is exclusively theirs; no more than the Christian church will justify herself by finding a province of works that are exclusively Christian.

This essay cannot elaborate the entire theology of Christ

[12] See Paul Tihon, "Religious and Secularization," in *Religious Brothers in Church and World Today* (Brussels, 1967), p. 13.

and church. We would hope that it at least indicates some
of the principles that must be examined as the continuing
background for all discussion on religious life. No one's
problems will automatically be solved this way; quite possibly their problems may seem to enlarge. But surely people are better off in the long run when they can begin to
sort out what are their real questions, doubts and fears.

It would seem, for example, that the real difficulty of
some people in religious congregations lies not in being a
religious but in being a Christian. If one can find it possible to remain a church member, it would seem relatively
easy to be a religious. This is not to say it is easy to see why
one should be a religious; only that it is difficult to see
why one should be a Christian. The person who says that
he wishes to leave religious life to become a better Christian might ask himself whether he would do even better at
being human by leaving the church.

The suggestion in the last paragraph is not meant to be
flippant. The logic of many people's positions seems to
lead in that direction. They complain that they cannot
serve mankind within religious life, but if they move out
of it they are often just as hindered by other "churchy"
obstacles. Some people may think it possible to remain
Christian while ceasing to be church members, but it is
difficult to see how Christianity can continue without some
historical community. If a person can find the sense and
the strength to stay in the church and work for her reform,
he might do best to stay where he is. The community one
is part of can no doubt become intolerable. Until that
point, the advantages of one's own community are: 1) it
already exists; 2) it is part of one's own history. Even
where a community is in need of great reform, an individ-

ual probably has more space to move and more leverage for change than he realizes. Presuming that the individual is going to stay in the church, the question for him is not whether anything is wrong with his congregation but whether there is another church community in which he can be more effective. If he thinks that no church group is worth staying with, he will then have to ask whether any non-church groups are having much notable success at community.

The individual who does not see sufficient meaning in his life should ask whether religious life is the root problem. If he is leaving from religious life, has he considered what he is going toward? The crisis of meaning today is spread throughout the whole world; some people in religious congregations might face that fact more squarely and become less obsessed with "problems of religious life."

This point is not meant to deny that there is a tremendous crisis of celibacy today and that this is a distinct though not wholly separate problem. We will consider the question of celibacy in the following chapter. All we must say here is that though a strong faith in God, Christ and church will not solve anyone's celibacy problems, the celibacy question cannot be dealt with at all unless such faith exists.

The vocation of man is to be man. Why anyone would take on the task of being a Christian is hard to say. Yet the world has profited from it sometimes in spite of the world's own antipathies and sometimes in spite of the Christian's failure to be human. In a similar way the church has profited from the existence of religious communities despite the frequent failures of members to be real followers of Christ.

3. The Community That Is Celibate

In his brilliant little novel, *Children at the Gate,* Edward Wallant describes the passage into adulthood of a young boy named Angelo. For Angelo, the world is a rational puzzle which he is striving to put together. There are two pieces, however, which do not fit. One is his retarded sister who awakens in him a depth of sympathy which goes beyond all reason. The other is a hospital intern named Sammy whose life fits no normal pattern at all. The funny and bizarre activities of Sammy on behalf of the human race eventually lead to tragedy. It is these activities which transform Angelo from a reasoning machine into a human being.

At one point in the story an old hospital attendant named Lebedov is accused of a shocking crime. What shocks Sammy is how terribly and unmercifully condemnatory everyone is toward old Lebedov. "People just don't realize," Sammy said in a musing voice. "I mean, go look at them talking, in palaces and laboratories and buildings. They get deeper and deeper in with their words, but they don't know. They get big cars, but they forget that they're so soft and frail that one teeny bump from their cars and they're nothing. They spend billions on fancy clothes, but underneath they're naked and only worth ninety-eight cents. They hide the earth from themselves with steel and formica so that they can forget that they're going to be buried in dirt. What they need is a big, big, tremendous joke to make them see the one little thing. They've got to remember Lebedov. He's a human—that's all there should be. There shouldn't be anything but people on this earth."

That was Sammy's concern, namely, that there should be people on earth. It sounds like an easy enough program to carry out, but something keeps going awry. The human race is obsessively concerned with reconstructing life piece by piece. In trying to do just that it ends up with something less than human. For the human person is not a construct of many impersonal objects. Human life must be grasped as a whole or else it is not grasped at all.

What is particularly needed in order that we should see the whole of human life, is a life that fits no pre-established program. The life that cannot be called normal challenges the meaning of normality and forces us to question the norms for human life. Fortunately, the human race does not need many poets, prophets and madmen, but it cannot get along at all without a few of them. By definition, most people fit into the general category of the normal; they thereby tend to equate the normal with the human. But the test for humanity is the acceptance of the abnormal which will keep our definitions of the human open-ended and receptive.

We spoke in the second chapter of the unusual vocation of being a Christian. This present chapter pertains to the more unusual way of life in celibate communities. By taking up the question of celibacy or virginity, we go straight to the heart of the issue. Celibacy is what structures this life into the various forms it has assumed. There is no doubt that celibacy has a basis in the New Testament insofar as there are those who have made themselves eunuchs for the kingdom of God (Mt. 19:12). Christ himself and some of his followers did not marry. The reason for this was somehow tied to the arrival of the kingdom in the last times which Christ was inaugurating. We shall see that the other two so-called evangelical counsels, poverty and obedience, are certainly in the gospels but they are used to characterize all Christian life. On the other hand, celibacy (which confusedly has been called chastity) obviously characterizes a smaller group of Christians.

The question to be raised here is not whether there were eunuchs for the kingdom of God in the first century, but whether celibacy has any value in the twentieth century. It is difficult to touch on this subject at all without sounding defensive. One of the most highly praised essays recently written on celibacy was done by Sidney Callahan in her book *Beyond Birth Control*.[1] It is ironic, to say the least, that a woman with six children has to give us the description of celibacy.

The celibates, for their part, have had to mute their claims. We have passed from an era in which marriage was said to be a good but less perfect state than religious life to a time when many religious seem to be saying: "We're *almost* as good as married people." Many married people may feel that the celibates are getting what they deserve. That may be so, but unfortunately, if we were to stop with this, the whole field of discussion would not have changed. The higher and lower terms would merely have switched places. What would be more helpful would be a new frame of reference for relating married and celibate lives.

One further prefatory remark should be made here. This

[1] New York, 1968.

chapter is not *the* chapter on celibacy; this book is a description of celibacy as a way of life. The title of this chapter is "The Community That Is Celibate." The accent here is on the word community and the kind of life that might be developed by a group of celibates.. It is very unfortunate that most discussions about celibacy in the Catholic church are in reference to the priesthood. One must admit that the question of clerical celibacy is of great importance insofar as a revolution in ecclesiastical structure would be initiated by a change in the requirement of celibacy. It is to be hoped that if the Catholic church changes here, it will carry through the revolution that Protestantism began. For what the church needs is not so much priests who are married but married men who are priests. In other words, the real change will be in understanding priesthood as a function within a man's own community, whether it be a marriage or celibate community.

We have almost nothing to say here of the celibacy of the secular clergy. At most there is a connection of appropriateness between church office and celibacy. On the other hand, celibacy is the very life form of sisterhoods and brotherhoods. It is extremely confusing not to separate these two questions as if the celibacy of sisterhoods and brotherhoods were a matter of legislated rule. It may be that sisters and brothers have little future in the church, but that future will not be decided by what happens to the clerical law of celibacy. One might speculate that the removal of that law would finally place the celibacy question in its proper context. It is not for us to surmise on the future of the secular clergy but, following a line of thought from Vatican II, if it survives it will probably be by incorporating the best elements of celibate community existence.[2]

The thesis put forward here is that the specificity of Christian celibacy lies in its communal character. Practically all religions and all societies have had outstanding celibates among their leaders. Most religious groups, for reasons not always the best, have prized celibacy as a way of life. The Christian church, too, has its share of lonely prophets. These are the men who have sufficient psychic strength to challenge the values of a whole society. If the church cannot always embrace such men, she should at least refrain from rushing in with a condemnation of them. Such men do need the support of others, even if it is only haltingly and from afar.

What the church as church brings to this area is a different kind of force: the celibate community. Inherent to Christianity is the recognition that we live in a social context that springs from the patterns of human institutions. One might not like some of the institutional elements in church and society today, but there is no way to change them without a social force. Institutions are changed by institutional pressures. The celibate community is to be a social charismatic, that is, a community that stands against the larger community for the latter's own good. Since it is approved by the total church, it need not stand under the control of any one man. As it is supported by the capabilities of each of its members, it need not place an intolerable burden on any one lonely man.

There are innumerable tasks to which such communities could put their energies for the good of church and larger

[2] Walter Abbot (ed.), *Documents of Vatican II* (New York, 1966), pp. 550 f.

society. However, there is one overarching mission that the celibate community has. When it is fulfilling this mission, the community will in the process find other meaningful tasks; failing this main mission, the community should cease to exist. This primary mission has never been clearer and never more needed than it is today. It is that the celibate group should be a demonstration of community existence in a technological and bureaucratic world. The demonstration can be quite striking when it is made by free adults in a relationship other than the marriage bond.

This mission pertains to the chief problem of our society. Can we find the way to let people be themselves and do what they choose to do, while at the same time have people live with each other in peace, justice and love? It would be naïve to suppose that anyone has the answer to that problem in some easy formula. It is in any case interesting to consider the contribution that the celibate community might make toward the solution.

The problem that we are becoming so acutely aware of today is our inability to let human beings be human. Spelled out more clearly, this means that we have a problem of segregation, followed by discrimination and domination, followed by suppression, mutilation and destruction. One repressed group after another comes before the television camera to plead for its right and its freedom. We are called upon to do what we can to ameliorate the conditions of each suffering group. At the same time we must be striving to get below the surface problems and find where the main suppression lies.

The contention in this essay is that the chief discriminatory problem pertain to women, or more precisely, to the relation of feminine and masculine. Could there be a worse case of class domination than that which puts one half of the human race subservient to the other half? Man dominates woman, which is not a good arrangement for women but is no better arrangement for men. The strong polarization of the race leads to the destruction in a man of those attitudes in himself that he associates with the feminine. Refusing to face the feminine stranger in his own make-up, man denies his own personal archeology. This process inevitably and increasingly leads to the domination of woman as sexual object.

The emergence of women to a status equal to yet different from men is surely the great task of our age. It would free for expression a whole spectrum of capabilities now latent in both men and women. It would free us from a narrow and obsessive concern with sex in order to let us be attentive to a variety of relational possibilities. There are some indications of such a movement in our society. The Christian churches often claim to have led the development of equalizing women. Undoubtedly there is some truth to this claim. However, to take a clear example of the length of the route yet to be traveled, the Second Vatican Council was hardly a shining witness to the bisexual character of the human race. As is true of so many social developments, the churches helped to initiate a movement but have failed to keep pace with its development.

The many rebellions that have been racking our society can be located in relation to this struggle for whole human persons in a whole human society. Uniting all the protests is a plea for trust in the human animal. There is a belief that human reality, despite all its problems, is a positive force which could achieve a better society if human freedom were trusted. One would have to be cautious about endorsing all the particulars of protest today. Nevertheless, is not the basic protest in favor of choice and variety a valid protest? Should not the church generally be on the side of creative minorities that break the stereotypes of the past? This tactic will probably not increase church membership but we have already suggested that that is not the purpose of the church. Is it not the function of the church to support all good things like sex, law or patriotism while being equally concerned that none of them is idolized?

In the sexual revolution that has been emerging on the horizon there is protest on behalf of whole persons instead of half-persons. To accept oneself as whole is to recognize a diversity of contrasting attitudes in oneself and others. Abraham Maslow has written: "It is as if less developed people lived in an Aristotelian world in which classes and concepts have sharp boundaries and are mutually exclusive and incompatible, for example, male-female, selfish-unselfish, adult-child, kind-cruel, good-bad. But seen by self-actuating people is the fact that A and not A interpenetrate and are one, that any person is simultaneously good and bad, male and female, adult and child. One cannot place a whole person on a continuum, only an abstract aspect of a person."[3] The most creative people, according to Maslow's findings, are those who combine what he calls hard and soft qualities. The question of these people is not whether to be hard or soft but when to be one or the other.

The celibate Christian community could act as one of

[3] *Toward a Psychology of Being* (Princeton, 1962), p. 35.

the protests against humanity in behalf of the whole of humanity. Its function need not be in proving itself better but in reminding everyone that things could be different. The value of a challenge which has a striking quality to it should not be underestimated. "One madman makes a hundred, one love makes a thousand," cries the man of La Mancha. The insane man reminds men of sanity and hopefully leads to a celebration of the gift of sanity. The powerful impact of the celibate community lies in the fact that its insanity—or at least its abnormality—is freely chosen. This might just be enough to make a man wonder: If people can clear-headedly choose this kind of life, then maybe there is something more to life than what I define as normal; maybe there is a beyond which I cannot see with my own eyes.

The celibate group, like all prophetic movements, stakes its hopes on the future. It testifies not to what is above life but to what is beyond death. "No faith is potent," writes Eric Hoffer, "unless it is also faith in the future; unless it has a millennial component."[4] To believe in the Lord Jesus is to believe in a community beyond death that can be sought for only by keeping the future open. The marriage community does the building for the kingdom of God, but not without relation to communities beyond the family unit.

The full approbation of marriage as the way in which most people are to find their full humanness must not lead to the hegemony of marriage over all human possibilities. It is not just the Christian celibate teams but a large segment of the human race that is in danger of getting excluded from adult humanity. Many people seem never to

[4] *Op. cit.,* p. 18.

have the chance of normal human growth. They are born retarded; they suffer early; they are cut down with injury. One need not go through the list of wounds mankind is subject to. The tendency of men is to judge that such life is not worth living: the function of Christianity is to remind men that human judgment is not final. One of the ways that the church can do this, particularly in this sexual area, is to have celibate communities that keep open the range of human possibilities.

Much of what we have said so far may seem hopelessly unrealistic considering the past and present organization of religious life. It must be admitted that there have been great obstacles to the celibate community fufilling the role described above. At times the religious order has seemed to move in the opposite direction, that is, it has carried on its own process of dehumanization by submitting people to rigid codes and static systems. This does not mean that everybody in the religious life of the past had the humanity squeezed out of them. There are too many cases one can point to of extraordinary personalities for whom the celibate life has honed to perfection their human qualities. Nevertheless, it is likely that the perfecting was traceable more to the power of healthy human flesh and the guidance of the Holy Spirit than to religious rules. In any case, without making any sweeping judgments on the past, we can say that the project for the future is to find the few people who can thrive in this life style and then give them full encouragement to grow in it.

These remarks on the power of celibate communities assume that these be people who can intensely love a small group and thereby love all people of both sexes. Complete segregation of men from women removes a whole set of problems but it also severely limits the possibility of growth. Since celibate groups are to manifest the widest range of human attitudes, the interaction of men and women is not only useful but necessary. Church celibacy for the future will only be meaningful if maturely chosen by people who can act maturely with members of both sexes. There must be occasion and provision for the forming of friendships between men and women. The human life of sexuality can be learned only in the living of it. There is no way for a man to discover the feminine in himself except by interacting with those who are feminine. There is no way for women to develop some of the more masculine traits except by acting self-reliantly with men.

A rapid evolution has been taking place in this aspect of religious life. The only question is whether it is too little and too late. It is to be hoped that religious life in the future will be so constituted as to enable people in their twenties to see and experience their possible alternatives. They will then choose either to marry or else to put their love at the service of a larger community that includes men and women.

The painful transition of the present moment finds many people in their thirties or forties passing through the adolescence of first romance. It is possible to postpone adolescence but not forever and not with impunity. One must go through adolescent experience, if not at eighteen then perhaps at thirty-eight; the latter being the more difficult way to do it. Many people who find themselves caught at this point today have little understanding of their own emotional life and even less realism when it comes to a consideration of other forms of life. Most such people are leaving religious life, often entering rather precipitously into married life. One can only hope that they will be happier with the change. Some of them might still be able to make a great contribution within the celibate community if they could find the way to integrate the new and overwhelming experience into their personal histories.

Deep friendships between men and women in religious life ought not and cannot be prevented today. What must be looked to is whether the relationships are open, calm and healthy rather than clandestine, contorted and desperate. The risk of illusion and naïveté is very great here because of the lack of experience and understanding. Proclamations that occasionally come down from on high to keep the doors locked and the rules enforced are quixotic attempts to solve a serious and delicate issue. Psychologists who are skeptical of the possibility of celibates forming very affective relationships must be carefully listened to. There must be restraints in such people's lives but the restraints must be discovered and developed by the individual out of the resources of his own life.

Two religious who lead from strength rather than weakness can achieve a powerful cooperative effort. Their relationship must have more of the qualities of friendship than that of marriage. However, some of the affective elements that should characterize all love may not be entirely absent. It would be the worst distortion of this suggestion to suppose that every man in religious life should go out searching for his thou to gain his experience. The relationship will be personalizing on both sides only if a partnership is evolving whereby the woman does not become a means of experience. The callousness of some men in such relationships can only be condemned. Yet even when there is good intention and genuine care, the woman is liable to great suffering in these relationships. The tendency of so many women to become involved in a totally absorbing way must not be overlooked in the friendships of celibate women.

Some people will feel that what is proposed here sounds feasible in theory, but in practice it has not worked in the past and will not work in the future. It is true that experience seems to go against the working model we are suggesting. It is not so evident, however, that this kind of atmosphere has ever been given a try. The future may indeed prove this wrong but there does not seem to be a past to go back to. There must be discovered new ways in which human beings can live and love. In some literature this has been unfortunately named "the third way." This term could give the impression of a movement half way from celibacy to marriage, as if there were a middle way. In writing on political parties in America, Michael Harrington has spoken of the need not for a third party but for a first party; what is needed is not someone at far left, far right or center but someone out front. When it comes to human love, we also need a first party, the movement of as many people as possible out front toward the future. The form of love is changing within marriage and outside marriage. The question for the celibate communities is whether they are ready to join the journey to the future. It will not necessitate a whittling away of celibacy but a richer, stronger, livelier, celibate love.

Celibate communities must encourage the individual to establish a variety of deep and lasting relationships with members of both sexes. Each person has to work within the limitations of his own person in determining how many people he can become deeply involved with and to what extent. Much of the failure in man-woman relationships in religious life is traceable to the existing community structure. In such relationships a strong supporting community is needed on both sides of the relation. Where the "community" is in fact mass collectivity, then a long retained conformity to system is no match at all for the surge of human emotion.

The celibate community is in a real testing time; the test is for survival. If religious life were to cease, something similar would have to arise. Our society badly needs a diversity of small social groups. The significance of these groups can be far out of proportion to their size. An individual cannot do the jobs nor can large and clumsy collectivities. We need small, autonomous teams federated within careful planning.

We have not tried to demonstrate the validity and value of celibacy. The proof, if there is one, is in the living of it. There will never be compelling theoretical reasons that can justify its acceptance by an individual. Apart from belief in a crucified and risen Lord it is impossible to make much sense out of it. In the strange world of the cross it might have a continuing validity.

To be a Jew or Christian is always a humbling task and often a lonely one. To be a celibate is to accept that kind of loneliness which accompanies imagination feeding upon social possibilities for a future world. In one respect, married and celibate are alike: They both have only faith, trust and love to stake their lives upon, while all the details of the future remain uncertain and can only be learned day by day.

4. Religious or Non-Religious

In these pages we have followed the standard terminology in referring to sisterhoods and brotherhoods as "religious life." There is no sense in pretending that this terminology does not now exist or that a new terminology can suddenly replace it. Yet we must at some point raise the question of whether anything better exemplifies the problem of religious life than the term "religious life."

Throughout the modern world the word religious has taken on more and more a pejorative meaning. To be called religious is almost as bad as being called pious. Of course, it will be immediately objected that religion and piety never were popular and never could hope to be. Christ was a scandal to his world, and his followers cannot wish for anything better. If the world ridicules us, this only validates our mission.

There is undoubtedly some truth to this rejoinder. Nevertheless, the modern antipathy to things religious is not to be dismissed so easily. Some of our contemporaries who are quite anti-religious are not "worldlings" in accord with the old stereotype. They are sometimes among the most honest, responsible and compassionate of men. One must also be a little suspicious about the religious minded who glory in their persecution. That the Christian's beliefs and practices may be laughed at is a possibility he must face; that he should cling to ridiculous beliefs and practices is not particularly to be encouraged. It is a good sign if Christians are ridiculed for serving their brothers with humility and love; it is a bad sign indeed if they conflict with the world because of their penchant for fourteenth-century styles.

This perennial question has come into much greater prominence in the last few decades. At least this is true of Protestant theology and more recently of Catholic theology although there is still very little evidence of the issue in literature on religious life. Since the Bonhoeffer eruption began a few years ago, the word religious has taken on a particularly bad meaning. Religion has become, in the terminology of some people, the opposite of faith and the great enemy of Christianity. To give the word only this meaning would no doubt be a case of overkill. A more balanced presentation of Bonhoeffer himself would show that he was most opposed to what in English we call religiosity. But there is much more to this contemporary discussion than either a confusion of theological words or a concern with worldly fads.

There is an important theme that is at issue in this discussion. It is not an entirely new theme, for it preoccupied the fathers of the church and the medieval theologians. There was a scholastic principle to the effect that the best of things can become the most corrupt of all. Man is capable of turning anything into an idol that obscures the living God. But nothing is so capable of idolization as that which stands closest to God. Religious practices should link man to God and yet they can begin to be trusted in as if they were God. Christ had the harshest words not for the weak human beings whom everybody else was condemning but for those who were apparently very virtuous and religious. This is not to say that virtue and religion have no place; it is rather to assert that if religion is not the great ally of faith it will be its greatest enemy.

All of this has been known since biblical times. What makes the issue so urgent today is that we stand at the end of centuries of idol smashing by the sciences. During this period the church has clung tenaciously to her religious beliefs and practices. The process may have been inevitable, but it was also inevitable that there would come a point when the church would have to make a decision. She must decide if she is going to drop some of the baggage from another century in order to set out on the perilous course of finding God in this century. Anyone who thinks that this step should not be taken might ask himself whether he really believes that "the earth is the Lord's and the fullness thereof." But anyone who thinks that this journey is not risky even to the point of possible extinction is more than a little naïve.

These introductory remarks are an attempt to give a balanced preview of what we believe about the secular. There is undoubtedly a process of secularization taking place in our world. Our reflections and suggestions concerning the need to move with this process are not made with boy scout optimism or Pollyanna enthusiasm. Our insistence on the need to get rid of the trappings of "religious life" is made with keen awareness that all change is not necessarily for the better and that the secularizing process is not an unambiguous good.

Our attack upon the use of the term "religious life" does not rest, therefore, on the supposition that religion is always bad. On the contrary, we defend the place of religion (that is, social expressions of belief, practice and worship) as useful and necessary to men. But precisely for that reason it is pretentious and arrogant to use the word "religious" as the distinguishing characteristic of celibate groups. In this good meaning for the word "religious," it is a quality that must be attributed to all Christians if not to all people who strive for fidelity.

In the negative sense of the word, "religious life" is even more inappropriate for the celibate communities. Religion (that is, a clinging to dead forms of the past) ought to be the last thing to characterize these groups. Even in the most traditional theology, the celibate groups are considered to be the forerunners of the advancing kingdom. If history is a secularizing process in which men free themselves of idols so as ultimately to be confronted by the living God, then the vanguard will be more secular than all the others. In short, although all men's lives are at present still mediated through religion, the Christian celibate communities ought to be the least religious of all.

There is obviously a need to sort out some of the terminology and give more of a theological basis for this last principle. To a large extent this discussion picks up the theme of chapter two. One cannot speak of the church as the community of believers who throw light on what God is doing without at the same time implying a notion of the world moving forward in time. Thus two of the liveliest issues in theology today are secularity and eschatology. Far from being opposed to one another, these two concerns can and should go together. We will briefly consider one and then the other before proceeding to make some reflections upon Christian sisters and brothers.

The word "secularity" is an artificially contrived word to give a qualified response to modern secular humanism. Like most invented words it will probably not be very successful and it will not even be helpful without some historical perspective and theological understanding. The word "secular" (or even "secularism") theoretically could function as a neutral word as in fact it did at its origin. Whereas "secular" first meant that something was not under the control of the church, the word quickly developed anti-Christian overtones. This tendency grew apace in the eighteenth and nineteenth centuries. By the twentieth century, secularism had become the rallying cry of the opponents of the church and the subject of stinging condemnations my church officials. Given this background, it should hardly be surprising that many people are confused by theologians now saying: The secular is good; anything religious is bad.

Part of the reason for the sudden reversal is a guilty conscience on the part of church people. They are of late discovering that they have been on the wrong side of many religious disputes. They have had to admit that some of the supposed anti-Christs were striving simply to improve the human lot. However, there is more to the renewed affirmation of the secular by Christians than a lot of breast beating over false accusations. Nor is it a betrayal of the gospel in favor of the world. It is instead the recovering of the double meaning of "world" in the gospel. The world is the place of sin and the power that holds man back from God. The world is at the same time the creation of God and the field of reconciliation. "God sent not his Son into the world to judge the world but to save the world." (Jn. 3:18). It is this "yes" and "no" to the world that we must consider in Jewish-Christian tradition.

What is claimed in this tradition is that God is to be found in the real, that is, in the world of human experience. There is an inevitable tendency on the part of man to trust in divine messages and oracles handed down at the beginning of things. Judaism and Christianity taught men to trust not in oracles but in God. And this one God is he who created the whole changing, struggling, confusing world. What he asks for is trust, the belief that he will see it through with man. If man would only stop hating himself and his brother, he could start using the possibilities available to him to build a better world.

It was thus out of a trust in God that man could come to accept the world, the time, and the humanity he had to work with. The question is not whether reality could be better but whether it is preferable to unreality. The choice is not whether or not to believe in a God but who is that God. Jewish and Christian tradition point not to a God above the clouds or a God mixed with the earth but to the God who confronted man at a moment of time and said: Do not be afraid, I will be with you.

The first step in changing the world is to accept the world as it is. Only when men can resolutely gaze at things as they are can they initiate changes to make them better. When they have stopped wishing that the past could be recovered, they can begin working for the future. Nothing has to be imposed on top of the world but the world needs encouragement to choose its own best possibilities and accept its own inherent limitations.

Faith in a God of history, therefore, is the affirmation of the world moving toward its own future. There is no neglect of sin and evil in this conception of the world. They are quite apparent as a counterforce in every attempt to affirm the emerging community. Because of fear, men constantly set up barriers that cut off part of the being that is human. Men are frightened of themselves and they are frightened by others. Therefore, they build walls of security and run away from their cowardice and ignorance.

The problems of evil, fear, hatred and ignorance have been with us for a long time and they remain with us today. What Christianity has claimed to be and what it could still offer to the world is a demonstration of what it means to affirm the human in the midst of evil and hatred. The Christian is to be that man with the compulsion to eradicate all the barriers of fear and hatred. But because no one is completely converted, there is a permanent danger of turning the church into a new ghetto, a new "we" against "them." This is exactly what the church must never be. The church must be a community open in principle to every person. A policy of segregation, whether racial, social or economic, is a flagrant contradiction of her nature.

Whatever work the church is engaged in, the primary concern must be the quality of the work and the life of the people. It is true that there is a level of size and external appearance that must be maintained for the survival of a social body. Without a continuing and coherent external pattern she would cease to have a "plausibility structure" that people could identify with.[1] Yet the church must believe that by going outward and maintaining flexible structures in response to the needs of the age, she will be a plausible sign. There may be something wrong with a church not growing in numbers; but a church that panics over diminishing bigness most certainly has something wrong with it. To become narcissistically obsessed

[1] See Peter Berger, *The Sacred Canopy* (Garden City, 1967), pp. 126 ff.

with her own self-survival is one of her greatest temptations.

The church's accomplishment of great deeds by size and power is not clearly guaranteed nor even clearly desirable. The more important question is whether mankind is moving forward by reducing the inhumanity of the world. "In other words, one should not lament the fact that others, such as the state or private foundations, have today assumed the great cultural, political and social tasks that the church in the past initiated and accomplished, and from which our civilization benefited before turning its back on Christianity."[2]

Looking to other agencies besides the church for the perfecting of the world has had its good effects even if the process is not without its own illusions and naïveté. Secularization remains an ambiguous phenomenon and it probably will until the end. A world "come of age" is not necessarily going to be a better world, but it will probably be much better or much worse. Man has become more capable of adult choices, of doing either great good or great evil. It remains to be seen whether mankind will perfect its own capacities for improving things or whether it will suffocate in its own progress. It is not entirely clear how or where the church can play a role in influencing this process for the good. But it is patently clear that the church can do no good by trying to get the world to return to the "age of religion." Proclamations to this effect are useless and self-defeating.

The reason that the church is tempted to hope for the re-establishing of Christendom is her failure to appreciate her own doctrine of eschatology. This doctrine is the other

[2] Gabriel Vahanian, *No Other God* (New York, 1966), p. 95.

side of the secularity question and the reason that there is a difference in the Christian affirmation of the secular. One hesitates to use the word "eschatological" because it is barren and confusing for so many people. Yet what is taking place around the word is a most interesting development. Whereas it was once true that the "last things" simply showed up last, today the end time has become the starting point and a dominating motif of theology.

It has been said in some recent theology that the layman witnesses to the "incarnational" and the religious to the "eschatological" aspect of the Christian life. This terminology has not been received with a great deal of enthusiasm in religious congregations. The distinction is indeed not an adequate one, but it may be that religious have rejected it for the wrong reason. "Eschatological" sounded other-worldly, spiritualistic and uninvolved. Since they seemed to be asked to leave flesh, society and time, it is hardly surprising that the religious showed little enthusiasm over the invitation. Possibly, however, they rejected something before they had understood it. It would be ironic if they were trying to escape their eschatological role just when eschatology is coming into style.

The affirming of the end time is the moving power of history and the basis of change. History progresses not by the application of self-evident principles but by a dream of the future. The God of Israel and Christianity is the power of man's future who calls men to more than a prolongation of their possibilities.[3] It is this promise that dominates the perspective of both Old and New Testaments. The difference in the New Testament is the belief

[3] Johannes Metz, "The Controversy about the Future of Man," *Journal of Ecumenical Studies,* IV (Spring, 1967), pp. 225–227.

that the person of the risen Lord is the beginning of the reign of *shalom*. If such a belief were always central, then the task of Christians would clearly be to keep moving forward toward the completion of that promise. "Not a flight *out* of the world, but a flight *with* the world 'forward' is the fundamental dynamism of the Christian hope in its renunciation of the world. This renunciation is therefore a flight only out of that self-made world which masters its present and lives solely out of its present, and whose 'time is always here' (cf. Jn. 7:6)."[4]

It is not a matter of having some elaborate "content" about the end of time. Christianity claims to know less in detail about the future than most ideologies do. What it does maintain is awareness that there is an end and that men cannot escape it by trying to forget it. Guilt, suffering and most of all death are just as real as ever, even though some humanism seems to pretend that they do not exist. Man cannot be free unless he faces this real situation with hope. "Human freedom is to live, to suffer and finally to die in this expectation. But before he dies, as long as the day lasts, man is free to work, to rise after each fall, to labour and not to grow weary. Whether or not we rise or tire depends on the use we make of our freedom to look to the end."[5]

The somewhat surprising consequence of this emergence of eschatology is the correlative concern with social involvement in the revolutions of today. The promise in Christianity is not a futuristic program but a community now being transformed. Instead of setting out a list of

[4] Johannes Metz, "The Church and the World," in *The WORD in History*, ed. T. Patrick Burke (New York, 1966), p. 80.

[5] Karl Barth, *Humanity of God* (Richmond, 1960), p. 83.

social reforms, Christianity casts before men the ultimate demand of God calling forth all human capabilities for action. Strangely enough, eschatological promises are always relevant in any age with their own peculiar kind of relevance. "The remembrance of the promise that has been given—of the promise in its givenness, not in its pastness—bores like a thorn in the flesh of every present and opens it for the future."[6]

The promise that has been given and the promise that now exists, exists in the flesh of a living community. God's promise *is* the people who are en route. They are sustained by the life that moves them upward and forward. A sacrifice for the future cannot be a sacrifice of men as a means to the future. Every now is the beginning future; it is now that action is needed. Social structures must be changed to allow men to grow into a future. The eschaton is not out there waiting for man; it is what man is to cooperate in bringing about. To be a sign of the kingdom is not to stand looking up to heaven but to join in God's revolution for the world that his kingdom may come.

The early Christians' two chief concerns converge in the notion of church: expectation of the end and universal mission. The expectation impels the mission; the mission is toward the expectation. Both of these combine to gather a community that is bound together by its looking beyond. Of course, in our era we no longer have a strong sense of the parousia's imminence but we are just as certain of its coming. Precisely because of its delay it is more important to point to its reality in the promise. This task of aspiring to the completed community is taken on particularly by celibate communities.

[6] Jürgen Moltmann, *Theology of Hope* (New York, 1967), p. 88.

The experience of the coming of the kingdom is the reason always given in scripture for the existence of celibacy (cf. Lk. 14:26; 18:29). "The general phenomenology of celibacy (as a special way of giving form to a certain awareness of value, and a vocation enabling one to devote himself entirely and specially to *this* value) becomes focused in Christian celibacy on a Christological, ecclesial, and eschatological significance, the three hallmarks essential to the value for which it was undertaken in the first place: for the kingdom of God."[7]

Various reasons are cited for celibacy. People speak of eschatological sign, entrance into community and functionality as if these were different and even opposed reasons. Actually, they are all the same reason. Contrary to the usual presentation, one does not get some mysterious call to be a virgin and later decide to live with some other people who have a like calling. The call to be an eschatological sign is the call to enter an eschatological community. The sign is that kind of community. If the eschaton is supposed to be a completed community, then one witnesses to it by entering a community trying to go that way. One joins a movement by getting in motion.

In similar fashion "functionality" is not an appendix but the reality. To ask whether celibacy is "merely" functional is to underestimate the importance of that which functions to make the community existence possible. People who ask the question are obviously worried about being turned into cheap labor for big institutions. But this is the opposite of the eschatological community's function. The puzzling phenomenon of the celibate group has the function of challenging the meaning of "functional."

[7] Edward Schillebeeckx, *Celibacy* (New York, 1968), p. 99.

Christ's preaching of the end time is always socially relevant in challenging men's conceptions of social relevance. The celibate group's social importance resides not in providing cheap labor but in challenging the notion that anyone (not just nuns) should be turned into cheap labor.

The chief characteristic of such groups should be their mobility. This is the way the group functions to be a witness to the eschaton. It is not the mobility of individuals who can be moved from one slot to another. It is the mobility of flight into the future. Not marrying is intrinsic to the way that the group attempts to set up a witness to the completed community. There is no necessary link between the renunciation of marriage and the witness to the kingdom, though the means are possible and are significant.[8] Married people can witness to this reality; celibate groups can fail to do so. Brotherhoods and sisterhoods simply intend this kind of witness more particularly and explicitly. The idea sounds good enough, but each individual must ask whether he can take the attendant risk of overextending himself. It has often been said that those who can find no human being to love devote themselves either to God or humanity. This is why it is so important that the group be the witness and not the isolated individual.

Despite the risks of individual failings and arrogant pretensions, such groups could serve a purpose. As history is more and more revealed in all its breadth and magnitude, the individual person may be overwhelmed by the process. It does little good to know how old or how great the human race is when trying to find some meaning in

[8] Karl Rahner, "The Theology of the Religious Life," in *Religious Orders in the Modern World,* p. 58.

one's own little life. Human beings need to be confronted with living people to decide on the truth of their own lives. High ideals and exalted principles cannot compete with living people even if these people are rather frail and fallible. The word "witness" is supposed to convey this sense of pointing to a value by participating in it with one's existence. Despite all the things wrong with sisterhoods and brotherhoods, the most important thing they have going for them is that they exist. They constitute a leverage of social change in a world where social leverage is utterly indispensable but often lacking.

This last point brings out what is most surprising for many people, namely, the connection between eschatology and social revolution. If these two are inextricably joined, then the signs of the kingdom are not obedient functionaries but loyal rebels. This is the appropriate renewal which is needed in sisterhoods and brotherhoods today. As we shall point out in chapter six, the religious congregation is not under the control of the local church official. The celibate group is to exercise a challenge to the official church. It is ironic that most Catholics would assume that religious life is the extension of the bishop. Its proper place is not under the finger of church office but out in front of it.

It is interesting to note that nothing has so infuriated reactionaries as to see sisters in the midst of agitation for social justice. To many people this seemed to be the ultimate inversion; the convent and social protest were the opposite poles of their world view. There is indeed an inversion here, but the confusion was in identifying nuns and children. The forerunners of the kingdom do not sit at home waiting for the parousia. It is at least debatable whether the priest, as part of the official church, should be too involved in the vortex of social change. One could not think of a better place for sisters and brothers to be.

These teams of loyal rebels would need the most flexible and fluid of organizational structures. What a ghastly error that "religious life" has been characterized by religion in the negative sense explained earlier in this chapter. The most visible thing about it has been its rigid adherence to dead forms from another age. It is difficult to recognize the agents of the future in the straitjackets of the past. The liberalizing changes grudgingly being made today are not going to help at all until this central issue is squarely faced. If people wish to be of the past, why change anything? If they wish to be out front in the present, then current attempts at adaptation are hopelessly inadequate. Moving from the 1890's to the 1930's in fashions simply makes one look a little sillier. If one wears sandals and a beard for a long enough time, one might eventually find himself in the avante-garde. But getting dragged by the heels into the twentieth century and being always just behind the times, one cannot even claim that he likes being different. To be ten centuries out of date is bad enough; to be ten years out of date is inexcusable.

The little to be said about religious habits is a fairly obvious consequence of the above. It should be emphasized that although the subject is hardly worth discussing, the issue is of the greatest importance. Liberals who try to convince conservatives that they should not object to this small change are missing the point. How a woman dresses should be a minor point, but that she should be allowed to dress like a woman is of the highest importance. The breakthrough on the habit, like negroes sitting at lunch counters, is only one small change—but it is the symbolic toppling of the whole system. Those who fight for total segregation, whether of negroes or nuns, are being realistic and consistent. Once a little integration is allowed, there is no telling where it will lead.

The question of religious habits epitomizes the failure to see that people must have the privacy of selfhood. A human being must be clearly distinguished from the external forms of the group. It should be emphasized that we are not trying to decide the question of sisters and brothers having distinguishing uniforms or insignia. Particularly for sisters doing some tasks, this might be helpful, possibly even necessary. Other groups wear their badges, caps or uniforms with pride and distinction; there is no reason why sisters and brothers cannot. Since presumably the eschaton is not in black and white, perhaps someone could design a multi-colored eschatological insignia.

The principle at stake, however, is an absolutely crucial one. A person must be allowed to step back from his role. When this distinction is not allowed, then the person's right to privacy is obliterated. No one can be on display all the time; it is simply inhuman. To be a witness to the public is not to be confused with being always on witness in public. A person must be allowed to be himself, enjoying at times the anonymity which is not only permissible but indispensable for human life. If one is always fitted into a stereotype, one cannot give a strong public witness because one has no private self to bring to it. Stereotypes, of course, do make the best cogs in the machines of total systems.

To the extent that the church fails to keep moving

through history toward the eschaton, she will fail to keep in proper relationship the public and private spheres. Everything will get turned upside down. The church then gets very worldly about other-worldly affairs and other-worldly about worldly affairs. She will plead spiritual detachment when it comes to housing laws for the poor, but she will use quite earthly means to see that her spiritual values are maintained. Likewise, it will happen that the public and private spheres are distorted by being reversed. Everything that should be made public is kept private; everything that should be kept private is made public. Thus financial policies or decision making is kept sacredly secret, but the life, conscience and personality of a sister are always stretched out on public display.

It would be easy to grow bitter on this point because the need is so desperate and there is such a horrifying misunderstanding of what is at stake, namely, the lives of people and the credibility of the church. So much of church matters that should be going on in clear public view is hidden behind closed doors. The attempt to hush up all the failings drives them deeper below the surface where they cannot be healed. The attempt to keep secrets becomes more and more inefficient with the advance of communication media. Far from solving the problem, however, this only makes church officials try harder and look sillier. Why cannot a public body speak its public mind to the public? If the church is going to claim to be greater than any secular organization, she will at least have to be as honest and straightforward as they are in public communication.

On the other hand, if churchmen are interested in preserving a sphere of privacy and secrecy in our world, there is plenty for them to work at. There is a tremendous lack of privacy in people's lives. Individuals should have the right not to be manipulated or have their lives pried into. The church, as defender of freedom, should indeed be standing in defense of this right. And if churchmen wish to begin protecting individuals from invasion of privacy, they might begin with sisters who are fighting for the right simply to be themselves.

5. Revelation and Community

In one of his recent essays, Karl Rahner wrote that a new notion of revelation emerged almost unnoticed from Vatican II.[1] What he meant, among other things, is that the last word is not said by the *Constitution on Divine Revelation*. A more developed notion of revelation is implied in other documents (for example, the *Declaration on the Relationship of the Church to Non-Christian Religions,* the *Declaration on Religious Freedom,* and the *Constitution on the Church in the Modern World*), but this notion has not become fully apparent. No one can clearly see at this point where the theology of revelation will eventually lead. We think it is possible, however, to suggest some implications for it in regard to the religious community, that is, the small autonomous group as distinct from the congregation.

The precise way in which religious life should be structured is not solely a theological issue. Most of what is proposed here has perhaps been said already by psychologists and sociologists. Nevertheless, it may be important to give theological support to their suggestions. Strangely enough, it is the theological notion of revelation that can easily be the obstacle to reform and progress. One finds that underneath a new terminology there remains a notion of revelation that is impersonal and objectified. The result of this deficiency is that creativity and autonomy are not whole-

[1] *Christian of the Future* (New York, 1966), pp. 96 ff.

72

heartedly endorsed. They are judged at the bar of an impersonal system out of the past. A properly developed
theology of revelation would tend to converge with the
findings of contemporary sciences. It is imperative, therefore, that we begin to understand Christian revelation as
personal rather than impersonal and social rather than
individualistic.

.A whole theology of revelation cannot be presented
here, but we must say enough to show that the issues are
not merely semantic. The change that has been taking
place in this area is not one of replacing words or filling a
few lacunae. It is more like the reversal of the whole endeavor, a starting from the other end. We have already
shown in chapter two what some of the consequences are
for ecclesiology. The same kind of shift occurs in nearly
every branch of theology. It is that peculiar kind of reversal in which the old is not destroyed but is somehow
subsumed in the new. But one must really let go of the
old before reaching the new synthesis.

In the first place, we speak of revelation as a present
occurrence. This is not entirely new, of course. The
church has always claimed to be the guardian and inter-
preter of a present revelation. What is different is not the
claim that revelation is present but that revelation is
present as occurring. In saying the latter, a real revolution
happens in that it becomes urgent to look at what is happening in the world and to use all available interpretive
tools to understand the present. Although the monuments
of Christian tradition may supply indispensable help,
there are no ready-made answers from the past as divine
revelation. The incompleteness of the revolution shows up
in the terminology of "revealed truths" (even occasionally

"revealed theology"). It is not quibbling to insist that
though the truths men speak may be revealing of God, no
truths have been revealed by God.

The insistence on the present character of Christian
revelation is not just a preference for one point of the
temporal continuum rather than another. The image of a
continuum is itself not a very good one for understanding
human time. The insistence upon the present is not a
negation of past and future but is instead an affirmation
of man. Man has a present (and presence) because he can
recognize his past and choose a future. It is inaccurate to
say that theology has overstressed the past to the detriment
of the present, or, as is sometimes said today, that the
present has been overstressed at the expense of the future.
Actually, the choice is between either a handed-down
thing which is outside lived, human time or an anthropology that unites past, present and future. The question
is whether or not to accept time, and this is the same question as asking if a real God speaks to real men in their
real lives. It is possible to misunderstand the meaning of
"present" but it is impossible to overstress it. By focusing
on the present as a communal movement toward the future, we do not disregard the past. Rather, we retain the
past in the only way in which it can exist: as sedimented
in the flesh and psyche of men who accept an historical
community.

The present as a quality of revelation is therefore an
assertion about the temporal but also about the social:
the presence of men one to another, the presence of man
to the world and to God. When we say that revelation
happens in the exchange between persons, we are not extending the meaning of the word or drawing a parallel.

We are saying that the primary meaning of the word pertains to what happens in the "in between." The reality is the relation; the meeting is the revelation. If the word "revelation" is used to refer to "what is contained in scripture and tradition," then this use is subsidiary to and dependent upon the present social reality. Persons reveal, and it is persons who are revealed; through being persons they reveal, and through revealing they become persons.

All of this may sound quite unorthodox to one who was taught that revelation closed with the death of the last apostle. It would indeed be difficult to say the above seriously without an adequate Christology. If Jesus of Nazareth is taken to be an oracle of divine truths, then we revert to a conception of human life that is controlled by propositions written long ago. But if in Jesus there is revealed something of the past, present and future of man's relation to God, then men must take up the search today. Belief in a risen Lord means that there is a way in which to hold together the record of faith from the past, the human resources of the present and the promise for the future. Revelation is the meeting of God with man. Christians believe that the supreme meeting point was, is and will be Jesus Christ.

The incarnational principle means that God is at work in all our endeavors. God reveals himself in the fleshly existence of each man. He is also revealed in the universal drives of a mankind that seeks to improve the cosmos. The one way he does not speak is in generalities to the general mass. He speaks in greatness and smallness, in concrete detail and ultimate vision. Religious life should presumably be a place attentive to this variety of expression. Unfortunately, contemporary religious life seems to be caught somewhere between the place where God murmurs in the heart and the place where he thunders from the mountain.

Much of the above description may seem irrelevant to the question of renewal in religious life. No obvious answers are forthcoming from the discussion, but that in itself is an important conclusion. The Vatican II decree on religious life urges as the basis of reform: "1) a continuous return to the sources of all Christian life and to the original inspiration behind a given community and 2) an adjustment of the community to the changed conditions of the times."[2] One can hardly quarrel with this admirable program of being attentive both to the Christian gospel and to contemporary society. The reform will be inadequate, however, unless there is developed a theology that will span these two points. It is useless to return to the gospel only to hack it into revealed truths that support the positions of general chapters. Likewise, there is no point in considering modern times if it is merely to adjust to it the well-formed system presupposed from the past. The gospel can be a brilliant light upon our present problem; the spirit of the founder may inspire us to continue struggling with the work. But the answers, if there are any, have to be discovered out of the experience of living people.

A theology of revelation could encourage us to trust in our own life history where the Spirit now works. Most religious congregations in this country seem to be awkward adaptations of something that grew up somewhere else. Even today the theology surrounding the life is largely an import that shows its European origins. Religious life is one area in which Americans could make a unique con-

[2] Abbot, *op. cit.*, p. 468.

tribution. It is in the American setting that one can find a sense of freedom, pluralism, organization, informality and social technique that could be invaluable for a thorough rethinking of religious life.

It is strange that we are so reluctant to trust in our experience for the renewing of religious life. God speaks American as well as Greek and German. This point is not made in a narrowly nationalistic vein. On the contrary, we are insisting on a breadth of vision that must be world-wide. However, there is nothing that we will be able to offer to the universal church if we do not work from an experience that is natively ours. The revelation met in Jesus of Nazareth leads us to believe that it is in the events of our own history that the God of all history is to be found.

With this summary of revelation as the background, we can now make some comments upon the meaning of authority in celibate communities. The larger aspect of authority, insofar as it pertains to the organized federation of communities, will be treated in chapter six. Here our concern is with the nuclear community of six or eight people. In a regional, national or international organization there necessarily develops a hierarchical arrangement of some kind. At the level of the local, sustaining community, a system of superiors is neither necessary nor helpful.

Church law has stipulated that every religious house must have a superior. It must be said here with the utmost clarity and decisiveness: a community by definition excludes a superior. Here is a crucial point where the religious congregation reveals not only how much it is out of touch with the modern world but how little it understands its own claims to be a community. A com-union is a sharing of life, a joining in partnership, a giving in reciprocity and a union of equals. It is conceivable that one could be superior to a community, but it is impossible to be a superior in a community.

It will be rightly claimed that the issue raised here is in large part one of language. In a community, someone makes decisions, someone exercises a leadership role, someone functions as liaison to the larger organization. The same person does not necessarily do all these things. In any case, the word "superior" is a most unfortunate term to refer to such appointed or assumed positions. Much worse is the fact that the language of sister superior actually represents the reality in many instances. One person in a group is given the impossible job (and then thinks it her responsibility) to test the obedience of others, to enforce rules upon people and to take other people's consciences upon herself. Many sincere superiors go to great lengths to exercise this responsibility in maternal fashion. The tragedy for them is that they do not understand that for many young adults today maternalism is only more infuriating than dictatorship. The early monastery may have formed itself on the image of the family with mother or father. To transpose this analogy to the apostolic congregation of today is no more suitable than using Paul's letter to Philemon as the Christian position on slavery.

It is sometimes said that the superior-subject relationship is almost unknown outside of religious life. This statement is quite inaccurate because vertical relationships of authority are in fact characteristic of contemporary bureaucratic structures. Nearly every businessman has a superior (though he may not call him that) to whom he is subject *in matters of business.* Everyone knows that outside of that clearly defined area this relationship does not determine their lives. Sometimes, of course, the relationship does extend beyond its proper boundaries. Sometimes business relationships either destroy a home life or destroy a man because he has no home life. Despite the frequent failure to make the distinction, the contemporary world is quite clear on the validity and necessity of the distinction.

What is implied in this distinction is the existence of two radically different kinds of human organization. One of them can be called a work-functional group; the other one is a personal-community group. Both of these forms of life are legitimate, but it must be noticed that there is a different demand and a different response appropriate to each.

In a functional group, men come together primarily as a means to something else. Men in a factory join their skills in a coordinated effort to turn out a product. There is nothing inherently wrong with this form of human organization. It cannot fully perfect human freedom, but it can nevertheless contribute to freedom's growth. If its possible good effects are limited, so are its bad ones. In a functional group, the following of inane rules may sometimes be the most sensible thing to do. It does not mean selling out one's conscience because one's conscience is not fully committed here.

The personal community, on the other hand, stands in sharp contrast to all of the above. Men are united not as a means to a further good but in the loving interrelationship of persons. If in this case the possibilities are greater, so are the demands. Whereas in a functional group we should not give ourselves in total dedication, in a personal community we must, Although the forming of the group is not for the purpose of turning out a "product," the life that overflows from such a community is highly productive for humanity. Every detail of life is of the utmost value, and one cannot in conscience put up with any legalistic or external control.

The tragic plight of religious congregations is not only that this distinction has not been effected; it is that the very opposite is often still preached as the ideal. There is strong urging, for example, that a man not be a religious and an educator but a religious educator, not distinguishing between the one aspect of his life and the other. This sounds like a lofty ideal but it fails to take account of the distinction between distinction and separation. Distinction does not separate, it unites; the failure to distinguish results in separation or confusion. A man's life should have some unity to it, but this can be achieved only by understanding how the different aspects of life are related. Thus one needs to penetrate lived experience with an adequate conceptual apparatus. The only other alternatives are to deal with life either by adding the parts together or by refusing admittance to any conceptual framework. Both of these lead to a separation that is destructive of life. People who are sure that they are dealing with the "whole man" are usually talking about a whole collection of inhuman pieces.

We are advocating a unity to life, but we are saying that unity requires a sharp and clear distinction between the personal community life of the celibates and the various tasks which they can accomplish in society. Because the distinction has not been made and because the congregations have been engaged in running large institutions, then the "community" came to be identified with the institution it ran. The word "community" then comes to have a meaning the exact opposite of what it should be. Those who talk about the supreme importance of the community are often those who have the least sense of what a community would be.

This confusion has produced a funny and incredible tangle of words in an argument now taking place in many congregations. The question pertains to the primacy of "community" or "apostolate." Those who talk in favor of community are often advocating more conformity to the regulations of "common life." The result of this conformity would be harmful to personal community but efficient for the institution. On the other hand, those who are against this position are forced into speaking for the primacy of the apostolate. But what they mean is a richer variety of apostolic tasks that spring from a more personal community. The result of this reorientation would be detrimental to current institutions but helpful for community. In short, although the categories doom the argument from the start, it would be a little clearer if those who argued for community argued for apostolate and those who argued for apostolate argued for community. It would be better still if it were recognized that there is something wrong with this kind of question when it is morassed in its own words. The solution, however, is not found in just mouthing the platitude that community and apostolate should always go together. The need is to admit the distinction of two aspects and then carefully examine the nature of each of them.

Recently, there has been a tendency in religious congregations to have two different people function as head of

the institution (for example, school principal) and superior
of the community. This is a good start, but it is likely that
it is seen simply as a division of work. What ought to be
seen is that the move is indispensable because there is question of two different *kinds* of operation. However, when
the division is well executed and if the community is small
enough, the "superior" will begin to wonder what he is
supposed to do. There does not seem to be any role left
for him. The answer quite simply is that the superior can
cease to exist. When the individual celibate is at work in
an institution, he should obey the commands of the chief;
his competent superior has the right to obedience in the
operation of the institution. When he is at home with
his brothers, then no one is superior (unless God wants the
title and his activities suggest he would not).

Some of the great decisions that affect the celibate's life
will not be entirely under his control, but that is the fate
of every human being. What will be under his control will
be all the small details of his interaction with others. For
a man's dignity and self-respect this latter is more important. Alexis de Tocqueville, with his customary perception, pointed out this paradox of freedom: "I should
be inclined to think freedom less necessary in the great
things than in the little ones, if it were possible to be
secure of the one without possessing the other."[3] The
legislating of big decisions is not nearly so destructive of
people as the control of small details in their lives. That a
corporation decides to move a man across the world can
be limiting to a man's freedom; that an adult human being

[3] Quoted in Robert Nisbet, *Community and Power* (New York,
1962), p. 258.

should have to ask permission to leave his house is utterly destructive of freedom.

Some people will think that this conception of community is opposed to the "vow of obedience." Undoubtedly there is a need to rethink the whole concept of obedience, and probably to do away with anything called a "vow." However, even in the traditional meaning of the "vow," it is not a giving over of one's will to a superior. The vow is a promise made only to God by which a person agrees to enter a "life-form" in the church. Obedience is directed to God according to the way the life is structured. It was once said that the voice of the superior is the voice of God. This was not entirely false insofar as everything can be the voice of God, though nothing is absolutely guaranteed to be so. No one can be relieved of the responsibility of listening attentively to the call of God that comes in the polyphonous modes of nature, history, the neighbor and one's own emerging being. In the notion of community proposed here, there will remain plenty of obeying to do, but it will be done by the *group* and carried out by the individual in relation to his community. The community's task is to obey the mission it has by going out to the world that needs its help.

The sharp distinction between the task and the community allows us to avoid a romantic anti-institutionalism. We recognize that for better or worse the modern technological and bureaucratic world is here to stay. Incredibly complex tasks must be handled lest the conditions of individual freedom disappear (for example, everyone strangling to death on soot). Our world is underdeveloped institutionally to deal with many regional and international problems. The tragedy of today's anti-institutionalism is that it always engenders worse institutions.

It is if anything more true of the Catholic church that she is under-institutionalized in the institutional side of life. If the church is going to function institutionally, she ought to do it efficiently. If money is going to be collected in church, then there are better ways to count it than having sisters spend their Sundays in doing the job. Institutions need the leadership that comes from intelligent, competent, strong-willed men who know how to set policy and who can get a job done. A Christian incarnationalism implies that the power structures of modern society are within the human framework that is to be accepted and transformed. One's hands may get dirtied in trying to do the work, but one cannot take away one's hands and keep them clean. To leave things as they are would be to leave them inhuman.

To keep the enormous bureaucracy aiding human development, there is need for a community life that sustains and refreshes the human being. Far from doing away with the personal community, modern organizations have made it desperately necessary. By separating himself from nature and constructing an artificial world, man is thrown back upon the uniqueness of human community. "Under these conditions, human encounter takes on new importance because of its starkness. Outside nature, men are all alone —but they are all alone together. They are more obviously than ever one another's context."[4] In this regard, a celibate group that actually lived by human encounter would be more relevant to society than was ever before possible.

The religious house is supposedly such a community in

[4] Walter Ong, *In the Human Grain* (New York, 1966), p. 133.

which each member supports all the others. But because of a failure to make the distinction sketched out in this chapter, the "community" tends to be a bureaucratic organization which by intention excludes deep, personal communication. The question of size, first of all, must be realistically faced. There cannot be close contact with one hundred people in the same house. A group must be small enough to have such a network of interrelations that the absence of one member is felt by all the others.[5] It may be possible to increase numbers, but it is doubtful that any operational and effective exchange is going on without previously having smaller groups or continuing to have sub-groups.

No one should naïvely assume that all the problems of community existence are solved once there are small groups. What the small group does is reveal the deeper problems and pose to us the question of whether we can cope with them at all. The small group will have more irritants and more personality problems; the one consolation will be that the problems are being faced instead of being hidden. Many administrators in religious congregations will frankly admit that they prefer large houses because the problem people are less difficult to take in the atmosphere of partial anonymity. The demand for anonymity, we have pointed out, is not an illegitimate one. But it is being found in the wrong place, and it is not being complemented by a real community support. Perhaps there would be fewer problem people if the distinctions proposed here were implemented. It may be that people cannot bear living in groups of six; but it is an inhuman solution to put them in groups of sixty.

[5] See Tihon, *op. cit.*, p. 13.

Many people cannot fathom what the words "divine revelation" mean because they have never experienced any human revelation. Their experience has always been on the level of the conveyance of impersonal fact. They have never crawled inside someone else's skin to see how the world looks from there. They can remain serene and stable, calm and objective because they have learned never to get involved. It is a position not without its advantages in avoiding pain and hardship. The price is hidden, but it is nonetheless high: a person's own humanity.

For revelation to occur between human beings, a set of conditions is usually necessary. These conditions include time, trust, love, shared experience, common interests and mutual concerns. Religious communities ought to be places consciously intent on bringing about these conditions. Religious life ought to be the place where the loving knowledge of revelation would most certainly be found. The tragic fact, however, is that many people in religious life are desperately lonely. It is to be hoped that those now growing up in religious life will for the most part avoid this problem. In reference to young people, it is not difficult to imagine what might be done through small group interaction and high level intellectual training. Thus would be encouraged a full human development that includes the growth of deep personal friendships, the expression of ordinary emotional affection and the acceptance of healthy, heterosexual relationships.

The problem appears much more acute when one looks at the present membership of religious congregations. What can be said of the older generation? There has always been a gap between generations, although it has probably increased in recent years and probably will get worse before it gets better. The gap between generations may be considerably bridged in the future, but for the moment it constitutes a very large problem. The wide age span in a typical religious community is a big obstacle to the formation of the close, personal relationships urged above.

Before religious life despairs of coping with the generation gap, three points should be made. 1) It is often remarked, but it bears repeating, that the split is not mainly one of chronological age Some of the most reactionary people seem to be those in their early thirties; on the other hand, there are people in their sixties and seventies who are marvelous in the capacity to face change. 2) The religious congregation cannot abandon the attempt to bridge the generation gap if it is to function as a model community. Our technological age badly needs the attempt even if the attempt is not wholly successful. How many other people in the modern world are even giving it a try? 3) The religious congregations are probably doing much better at the task than they give themselves credit for. If the difficulties of living together and talking together are acute, at least the problems are being faced. Every human organization is untidy and frustrating when one sees it from the inside. A truly personal community will reveal all the more of human failure, fear and frustration precisely because here they can be borne with and partially cured.

The problem is not really so much the aged as the unloved. The world is filled with people whose capacity to love is atrophied. For many of them, it is a failure for which they are not culpable. The Christian is called upon to give his love particularly to the unloved; they, too, in their own way are a revelation of God. "People can be so broken and so hurt that they cannot love and they need to be cherished and reassured until they can. One of the responsibilities of the church is to be on the alert for those people who later in life need the love and reassurance they should have had when they were younger."[6]

The religious life has its share of lonely people who have not experienced any deep human affection. This constitutes a problem for the would-be reformer; one cannot phase out people. In all attempts at reform there must be provision for options and real respect for convictions. Many of the aged, the sick and the emotionally crippled cannot experience the call for radical reform as other than a threat to their very existence. If one cannot hold up progress on their account, at least one can be sympathetic to their problems.

Perhaps those who wish to make big changes could work at the conditions that allow for change. A certain objectivity might allow for smoother change and fewer people getting hurt. When someone has evidently staked his life on hundreds of rigidly held rules, the process of change seems utterly stymied. Yet it is not necessary to change his mind on all of them. It is only necessary to convince the person that other experiences will indeed hurt but they will not destroy. The reformer may not be wholly trustworthy but it is necessary for him to convince the other that it is all right to trust another person.

6. Sharing in the Lord's Power

In the previous chapter we have restricted the consideration of authority to the local level. We have asserted that the community by definition excludes a superior; furthermore, that the community is to be the unit of autonomy, power and obedience. Far from doing away with all authority structure, this development would make more imperative the need for intelligently planned structures for decision making. The federation of local communities cannot be achieved without the adoption of the best techniques of the contemporary business and government world.

It is often claimed today that the New Testament idea of authority sharply distinguishes the meaning of authority in the church from authority in the secular arena. There is a solid exegetical basis for this contention, but to stop with this claim might be misleading. 1) An evolution in the notion of authority has taken place in the secular sphere. This has happened particularly in Western countries during recent centuries, but the change has spread rapidly to all parts of the world. To what extent the change in the secular is traceable to Christianity's influence is a debatable point that we will not consider here. 2) Insofar as Christianity goes beyond the local community it is necessarily involved in secular structures which must be developed by intelligent and industrious men. The acceptance of the gospel as a message of love and service guarantees no success in managing a world-wide church. 3) It follows that Christians had better tread lightly in comparing the gospel notion of authority and secular power. We would agree that the universal church should not stop with the notion of authority developed in secular society. The problem of the present, however, lies not in the church getting beyond secular notions but in the church getting so far. At the level of the personal community, the gospel ideas of love and service can be immediately implemented by any two or three gathered in his name. But when one considers any larger church, it becomes a different issue. Christians should not only refrain from condemning such things as constitutions, checks and balances, voting and so forth, but should begin learning how to bring these into the church.

There are, therefore, two opposed notions of power, authority and law, but it is inaccurate to designate them as Christian and secular. The church is ineluctably caught up in secular political structures. Her job is to find the best ones available. Likewise, secular powers at their best have some of that character of authority which the gospel urges. A delicate tension will remain here, and the Christian is never entirely certain that he is not selling out the gospel to a sinful world. The church can never wholly embrace the world nor can she ever condemn it. The Christian cannot trust himself to worldly power, but it would be just as irresponsible to flee from it.

The *Constitution on the Church* produced by Vatican II is a blueprint for rethinking the church's authority structure. It does not set out the details of what this means for religious congregations. However, by putting the question into a biblical-theological understanding of church, it is more helpful than the decree on religious life. We shall make some comments on the ideal of authority held out for the human race and the ways the church might aid the world in its striving toward it. A few explicit applications to religious congregations will be made in the latter part of the chapter.

In a lucid essay at the time of the Council, Edward Schillebeeckx described the work of the Council as a process of decentralization (or decentration).[1] He sees this taking place in a five-fold movement outward: 1) from church to Christ, 2) from pope to bishops, 3) from hierarchy to people, 4) from Catholicism to other Christian churches, 5) from Christianity to the non-Christian world. The advantage of this breakdown is that it shows the full context of particular changes. It indicates, for example, that the collegial structure of the episcopate is one obvious step among others.

The disadvantage of referring to decentration or the decentralizing of authority is that it catches only one-half the process. The term is, therefore, very misleading. Throughout our society there is great need for a process of change, part of the process being a greater *centralization* of authority. In government and education, as well as in the church, we need more centralization of some aspects of life in order to make a decentralization of other parts of life possible. People who fight only for the latter do not see that the former is a necessary part of it. For example, the local community gaining the responsibility for schools is possible only with better planning and

[1] *Collaboration of Religious among Themselves, with the Episcopacy, and with Secular Priests* (Chicago, 1965), pp. 3–28.

financing. Giving authority to the people for their schools would require a strong regional power to make it effective. Similarly, eighty thousand local governments in the United States do not represent local authority. The proliferation of municipal governments threatens local responsibility. To decentralize power to the people there has to be found a way to unify and centralize the sprawl of government operation.

Those who defend individual rights by attacking centralized authority are hurting their own cause. One cannot save individual rights by destroying the main power center, but only by forming *groups* that will make power operative at every level and keep it human by its interaction with other power groups. An authoritarian ruler, even if he wished to, could not turn over authority to the masses. He can decentralize responsibility only as the isolated individuals form groupings that centralize power, planning and operation.

An individual can be properly responsible, therefore, only when he is in a well-unified and centralized body in which there are intermediate structures for accountability at every level. Most authoritarians cannot stop being authoritarian until they get some authority. Bishops who misuse power will stop doing so not when the laity weakens their power but when their brother bishops function as a group to *strengthen,* direct and correct the use of power. A colorful American priest, when told at the Council that the great reform was to be an increase of power for bishops, commented: "Get more power? They already have enough to hang us." What this priest did not recognize was that a bishop without constitutional or collegial safeguards is in a more helpless and isolated position than the priest.

And the top man in Rome, given all the power and no subsidiary structures in the church, would be in the most isolated and precarious position of all.

The "decentrations" listed above, therefore, are not the giving away or the destruction of power by the first member in each of the five pairs. The movement from the first to the second element is precisely to bring out the full reality of the first so that the first can better give and receive. When discussion began on the collegial character of episcopacy, some people opposed it on the grounds that it would reduce papal power. But the true friends of the papacy are not those who try to make the pope increase by making everyone else decrease. The Petrine office would be destroyed by making the pope a ruler and the bishops his functionaries. On the other hand, the papacy could be of great service to the church if it emerged at the *center* of a strong episcopal college. The paradox is that the decentralization from papacy to episcopacy means, among other things, a stronger centralized power for the pope.

It is evident in the last statement that there are two meanings of power being talked about at this point. The giving up of power to rule is what enables a man to acquire the power of love and service. It is not a mistake to use the word "power" in reference to the latter. Anyone who thinks that love and service are not powerful has not grasped the gospel message. This power is not just a pale image of the power to rule. Admittedly, the former cannot historically function without some of the techniques developed by the latter. But love and service ought to be the ideals for which all structures are developed in the church.

Christianity claims that man cannot find himself except

through and with others. The highest realities can be possessed only in giving them away. The gospel is not so much a doctrinal exposition on authority as a demonstration of love and power, obedience and freedom in the life of Jesus. He reveals in his life the triune God in whom a single divine power is shared with order of precedence but with no taint of slavish submission. In the giving up of his life Jesus attains all power in heaven and on earth. Christianity is not a religion in which the means to order men's lives have been bestowed upon a few rulers. It is the unique religion in which God transforms the community from within. What Christianity offers to the world is received by Jesus Christ who came both from the Word on high and the community of mankind. God's power has been decentralized to all men by being centralized in the man Jesus.

The Second Vatican Council, by placing Christ at the center, at the same time asserted that the whole church in every member shares in the life, power, priesthood and prophetic office of the risen Lord. It is simply not true that there are those who possess "Christian things" to be distributed to those who do not possess them. It is not true of Christ's relation to the apostles, nor the pope's relation to the bishops, nor the bishop's relation to the people. Rather, power is centralized in *one;* it is shared by *all.* Those who are ordained or appointed to office are those chosen to serve all their brothers that they might all come to recognize the one God.

If the ultimate ideal is a community of free men, then the giving of commands and the obeying of commands become slightly different means for building up the community. To obey in Christianity is to listen and respond;

to govern in Christianity is also to listen and respond, but from the more general point of effecting a decision for all. The bishop is the master listener in the church; he does not have to make decisions by majority vote of his people, but he has to listen to the Christian tradition as it sounds through the lives of Christian people. No man in our society has competence in every area of life; what he must do is draw upon and draw together the competencies of many people. The leader must not only listen to those who bring forward information and projects but also seek out those who are particularly competent in some area. It is not a denigration of the episcopal office to propose that the best of human resources be made available to those in authority. The bishop is not the chairman of a business corporation, but he ought at least to have available the good human techniques developed in the corporation world. At the same time, he must retain or recover the sense of inspiring, prophetic, priestly leadership that men still look for today. Computers have not replaced people; they have instead demonstrated that we need leaders who are clearly distinguishable from machines.

It is one thing to be generally in favor of a social structure of dialogue and responsibility; it is quite another thing to achieve this in practice. It is naïve to suppose that if each person is of good will and does his best, then all problems will take care of themselves. The social structure, especially in a complicated society, is never morally neutral. "Structured evil is one of the new discoveries of our day. Structured evil refers to the conditions that obtain when people in the organization by conforming to the existing rules are prevented from striving for happiness which is our human right. We used to think that

evil was disorganization.''[2] This does not mean that disorganization is preferable to order, but only that there are
many ways to get order and that all of them are not
equally good. The issue is not whether to have order or
chaos but how we are to strive for a truly human order.
There are premature ways of getting order in which problems can be hidden almost indefinitely. If the church
edges out her most outspoken members, and if the church
does not get involved in cloudy, controversial issues, a
beautiful order and stability can be achieved; but it would
be at the cost of becoming innocuous.

One does not get dialogue by having everyone talk; one
does not achieve democracy by having everyone vote on
everything. To have a dialogical society it is indispensable
to have adequate *means* of communication; to have a participant society, it is necessary to develop democratic
processes and subsidiary structures. A bishop cannot listen
to his people unless there is some practical means of listening. Men cannot offer their suggestions or complaints unless there is an efficient way to convey them. The church
cannot have a constitution (in the modern sense), since
she ultimately relies on the Holy Spirit. But this does not
eliminate the need for written norms, stated guarantees
and effective organizations. The organizations needed are
those that deal effectively with questions at the level where
questions arise. Such organizations are open upward and
downward. On the one hand, they make more efficient the
exercise of higher authority; on the other hand, they give
to individual Christians and to Christian groups a source
of strength and a right to redress of grievances. People

[2] Marie Augusta Neal, "The Value of Religious Community," in
Vows But No Walls, ed. Eugene Grollmes (St. Louis, 1967), p. 156.

who are prone to attack the juridical and institutional do
not see that they are also attacking constitutional accountability, due process and checks of power. If we are
going to continue to exist in the organizational world, we
will get rid of bad organizations only by creating better
ones.

The whole church is now in that painful transitional
moment of trying to create the intermediate structures
which are indispensable for a responsible exercise of authority. This is a difficult step in that one cannot simply
create operationally effective forums. Furthermore, the
groups that are immediately organized may seem to be
a help to communication; but at a later period they may
become a hindrance if they do not mirror a cross section
of the church. One cannot wait until everything is per-
fectly planned, but there is need for some careful planning
of authority structure and some defining of limits of competence. For example, a lay school board in a parish may be
no more competent and just as authoritarian as any pastor;
on the other hand, a regional educational board with laity
(including religious) and clergy might be a very helpful
move. Or, to take another organizational development, a
priests' senate may today be helpful and necessary in
dealing with questions pertaining to priests; care must be
exercised, however, lest this kind of body begin dictating
the educational policy that ought to be decided by a
diocesan council.

The church today is discovering what many other people
in contemporary society know, namely, that committees
give birth to subcommittees and that there is a danger
that the tangle of means will obscure the end. For a body
that has long defended the right to Sunday rest, it has a

strange penchant for working its own personnel through week-end conferences. Talking at conferences may get work initiated and may summarize work done, but it does not do the work. Dialogue might be increased by less talking and more homework. When one gets to the point of going to conferences three hundred days a year, one begins to wonder when he is supposed to think, read or just live. The talk mystique (often in reaction to a silence mystique) is part of an uncompleted revolution in developing a structure which is needed to make both authority and freedom responsible.

The religious congregation at the present is perhaps one of the best examples of incomplete democracy that tends to be self-destructive. Voting, for example, is not a cure for its problems. There is no sense in voting for delegates to a chapter unless at the same time there are platforms, campaigns and political strategy. Otherwise, the elections go almost invariably to the people who have been around longest in visible jobs and have not made any enemies. The power of the vote is lost if it is trivialized by meaningless votes on important issues or endless votes on meaningless issues. The age of authority and of spirited leadership is not over. We need people who, elected to office, can take the reins of leadership, listen to the people they are trying to represent and make intelligent decisions. This is not a time for voting on everything; it is a time for bold leadership.

The existence of the autonomous group does not do away with these larger organizational questions. As pointed out in chapter one, the question of juridical framework must not be dismissed (though for a time it may have to be disregarded). The church through the centuries has insisted upon a religious congregation having an approved, written constitution. To take vows is to enter a way of life that is constitutionally defined. A rule or constitution should exist not as a thing to be enforced but as a guarantee of the rights of the individual and the rights of the group. A person entering into life with a group ought to know the ideals of the group and the procedures of the organization. A society, in its turn, needs a way to specify responsibilities to members and deal with individuals who are not responsive. In the long run, this will bring about a more personal order than that which is achieved by assuming that everything should be run on an *ad hoc* basis with lots of good will.

Marriage is a contract from one point of view; this characteristic of marriage should not be done away with. Insofar as a marriage is successful, it will cease to be a contract, not because the contract is broken but because it is transcended in a life that is richer than contracts. A marriage in which one partner is always saying: "You have a contract with me, and therefore . . ." is not much of a marriage even if it never ends in divorce. In similar fashion we are defending the validity of a legal structure for religious life. The paraphernalia of vow(s), constitutions, rules could be greatly reduced, but that is not the main issue. The point is that they are necessary but that religious life should not be identified with any of them. The most successful vows will be those that are forgotten. Endless literature on "practicing the vows" is self-defeating. So long as the rights of the individuals and groups are not threatened, there is no point to talking about vows and rules. If there is any life in the body, it ought to demonstrate it by getting on with its task of loving God and humanizing the world.

There is little point in having a multiplicity of vows; the action is a unity. A "vow," in the singular, might be helpful, though perhaps the word "promise" would be better. The word "vow" has overtones which are difficult to escape from in any rethinking. However, it would be naïve to think that any great reform will take place with the replacement of "vows" by "promises." It may be misunderstood as simply a further erosion of what are already weakened foundations.

Whether any person should permanently bind himself in this form of life seems to be a debatable issue. It would seem to us that the ideal ought to be retained and that some people will decide to be life-long members. The place of celibate communities, as described in chapter three, would seem to necessitate a permanent corps of people. It should be evident that no one ought to be pressured into this kind of agreement until he feels that he can so commit himself.

There are in addition many young people who would be willing to associate themselves with these teams for a few years. This is in fact already an established pattern, but the religious congregations have not admitted it. Because the congregations do not admit what is happening, they suffer several unfortunate consequences. 1) There is still a barrier which one crosses on entering and a much larger barrier one must cross in leaving. Particularly for women, it can still be a traumatic experience to go from convent to "world" instead of a quite normal one. 2) The congregations are taking upon themselves an economic burden they cannot handle. The education they provide ought to be "on the job training" for younger people and time off for older people. Instead, the young person is supposedly in the congregation after a novitiate year; he then receives thousands of dollars of education and often leaves as soon as he is ready to begin. This process is not one of dishonest intent; it is simply that the education often prepares people to leave. 3) Because the congregation maintains a clear boundary of in and out, many people who leave do not retain any relationship to the congregation. If the religious life were a series of concentric circles, people who leave the small celibate team might simply move toward the outer rim but retain a relationship. Perhaps new forms of communal existence would grow up among people who retain some association. There have long been third orders, auxiliaries, associate members and so forth, but these have seldom functioned in real partnership. Small groups of married people living in some structured community have never proved very successful. But who can say that all the possibilities for this have been exhausted?

The key is the ex-member who has almost never played a part in associations because he had to appear as "defector" from his vocation. Individuals who have left the celibate community ought surely to be considered friends and associates rather than renegades. This kind of relationship is, of course, already operative at a personal level, but it lacks official endorsement. As with many other suggestions, we admit that this blurring of who is in and who is out is a real threat to the continuance of the life. A social body to retain its identity ineluctably sets up criteria for distinguishing members and non-members. However, just as the "church" is today a multi-leveled word which can apply to different groups in concentric circles, so the religious congregation must dare to find itself while building no walls to separate member from non-member.

Another problem that would have to be dealt with is the movement from one local community to another. There should be a means built into the administrative machinery by which the local group could recommend a change of personnel or an individual could choose to move to another group. It is immediately evident that this would be a difficult, practical problem. We raise it here because it reveals the bigger question of how a local group is to retain autonomy, including veto power, and yet function within a federation. This is a very old problem that has never been fully resolved whether in regard to the federal government, labor unions, boards of education or the United Nations. The tremendous difficulty of the undertaking must not stop us from continuing the attempt to develop genuine federations. Strong central leadership and autonomous local chapters are not incompatible; they must go together. But the job requires more intelligence, experience, courage and technique than the human race has usually had available.

It should be carefully noted that the problem of unity with diversity is not essentially one of size. Once there is a large organization, then the problems of structure are essentially the same. Granted that it will be more difficult to perfect an organization for millions of people, the same problems exist at a lower level. When a sister says that her congregation is too big and that it must be broken down before it can be renewed, she is missing the point. Size may be one of the few things it has going in its favor. A congregation of two thousand that is not going anywhere would only multiply its problems by splitting into four or five separate units. Of course, four or five regions in which regional councils had real authority would be quite another matter. The basic problems remain: centralized leadership and decentralized responsibility.

The problem is not so much freedom as dignity and communication. Most people recognize that they cannot control all the decisions that affect their lives. They know that freedom is exercised within severe limits that they themselves do not choose. What the individual wants today is to be respected as a personal being who can voice his opinion when he is knowledgable and who can participate in decisions when he is competent. He does not wish to dialogue incessantly on intramural trivia, but he does want available means of communication so that he can pass on his specialized information. He does not wish to vote on the Sunday menu, but he wishes to have decision making include his contribution on important issues.

The desperate lack of communication in our society will only be overcome with tremendous imagination and skill. When an institution disintegrates from lack of communication, people wonder what caused it. But there is no need to assign a cause to the failure other than that no one succeeded in overcoming the enormous communication gap that exists in modern institutions. The means used today are nearly always inadequate and left over from another age. After a short time in any institution, most people give up listening to loud-speakers, looking at bulletin boards or reading anything on ditto paper. Someone keeps sending messages with the hope that if there are enough of them they will get through. Most teachers did not have any difficulty identifying with Miss Kaufman's caricature of school communication in *Up the Down Staircase*.

We are simply noting here that the problem of communication is endemic to the modern world. The religious congregation, if it is going to claim to go beyond its society, must put its best efforts to dealing with the problem. It may already be succeeding as well as any group in our society; at least its administration is still *someone* and not a recorded announcement. But in addition to having humane leaders and autonomous groups, it must continue to work at creating intermediate structures that aid communication and diversify power.

The religious congregation continues rightly to claim the "privilege of exemption," that is, it is not directly subject to episcopal control in matters pertaining to the internal working of the congregation.[3] The words "privilege" and "exemption" are both rather poor choices to describe the reality. The way of life is not so much granted as a privilege but asserted as a right. It represents a group of people expressing the priestly-prophetic character of all Christians. They give witness that the church exists not as a collection of jurisdictional units called dioceses but as a marvelous mixture of little churches. The word "exemption" does not mean escape from obedience but a wider responsibility to the church in her universal mission. The religious order is not controlled by the local bishop so that it can be a forceful challenge to the bishop and make a contribution at the level of the episcopal college.

This charismatic function belongs to the Christian community because it is Christian and not because it is handed down by the hierarchy. It would be a blatant contradiction

[3] See Abbot, *op. cit.*, p. 422.

for the congregation to make this prophetic claim within the church and then make the internal working of the congregation the opposite of this. The "exempt" character is meant to perfect the free obedience of all by allowing each to share in the building of the body. An institution which has no effective subsidiary structures makes any prophetical rising from below a practical impossibility. There is inevitably a disrespect for the freedom of the person unless there are means for the higher to listen to the lower and unless there are ways in which those on a lower level can exercise genuine initiative.

The job for religious congregations, therefore, is to create the structures necessary, concentrate on the positive ideals, and let people at each level make their own decisions. In its *Declaration on Religious Freedom,* the Council made no exception for people in religious life when it declared: "Therefore, this Vatican Council urges everyone, especially those who are charged with the task of educating others, to do their utmost to form men who will respect the moral order and be obedient to lawful authority. Let them form men too who will be lovers of true freedom—men, in other words, who will come to decisions on their own judgment and in the light of truth, govern their activities with a sense of responsibility, and strive after what is true and right, willing always to join with others in cooperative effort."[4]

[4] *Ibid.,* p. 687.

7. Freedom of Sons and Daughters

Much of the material in the preceding three chapters centers around the key theme of freedom. That is, the secularizing process, insofar as it is a valid process, is a liberating one. Likewise, the establishment of model communities on the basis of Christian revelation attempts to provide the context for free persons. Finally, the institutional restructuring recommended in chapter six is for the sake of growth in freedom.

It may be helpful at this point to draw together these strands by analyzing the notion of freedom itself and relating this notion to religious life. It is a massive topic for which there is no adequate definition. "Any one who has pondered the problem of freedom and determinism will probably sympathize with the sentiment which prompted Milton to assign discussion of this topic to some little devils in Satan's legions who liked to bandy it about during moments of relaxation—without getting anywhere."[1] Aware of the great difficulty of treating the topic adequately, we nevertheless must attempt some description of freedom.

Man is the being who desires to be free; freedom is the goal and the task of man's life. Precisely because it is the goal of human life, freedom cannot be comprehended antecedently; it is understood only in the process whereby

[1] David Roberts, *Psychotherapy and a Christian View of Man* (New York, 1950), p. 94.

it is attained. Men seek diligently and desperately for freedom but they are only vaguely aware of what they are seeking. It is not surprising, therefore, that in contemporary literature, or on the contemporary street corner, there are few words more frequently used than the words "free" and "freedom." At the same time, however, there are few words more ambiguous in meaning and more constantly misunderstood.

It should be fairly obvious, though it is seldom made explicit, that there are numerous meanings for the word "freedom." They correspond to the different levels at which freedom exists. Christians often claim to have the final word on freedom and to speak of freedom in its most perfected form. But they cannot, on this account, neglect the other meanings and levels of freedom. Our description will move through several of these different meanings.

There is a first sense of the word "freedom" that applies to every man. Paradoxically, man's search is for freedom and yet he is already born free. Each human being is constituted by his ability to say "yes" and "no." Man can assent to determinisms that structure his life or he can refuse to accept them. Man is the creature who can say "no." Other creatures say "yes" by the necessary acceptance of existence; only man can shut the door. This fundamental capacity is not the freedom which St. Paul speaks of, nor is it the freedom which is sought for in the contemporary world. Nevertheless, we must not overlook or underestimate this capacity; it is at this deepest level that the freedom of the sons (and daughters) takes hold. Furthermore, precisely because this freedom is so commonplace, it is not sufficiently understood or appreciated by a large part of mankind.

What people almost invariably think of first is freedom at the level of external activity. Although this meaning of freedom must not be underemphasized, it must not be equated with the whole. The search on the operational level will be abortive unless it is accompanied by an inner movement toward freedom. Despite the fact that man can extend indefinitely his choices and accomplishments, he vaguely senses that he is not attaining thereby the freedom he desires. Those people consciously intent on gaining freedom are dismayed to find that every choice is limiting, that every object and indeed the totality of objects does not satisfy the quest, that every triumph over the tyranny of nature exposes man to the tyranny of human whim and passion.

It is not so surprising, therefore, that many people give up the struggle and escape from the unbearable burden of freedom. They submit to the living of their lives mechanically, exchanging for the temporal process the unchanging patterns of their own minds. For those people, on the other hand, who refuse to escape from time, freedom can become a curse and a condemnation. Whatever else one may think of this latter view of freedom, it is at least one that is aware of the mystery and the frightful risk of freedom. "I didn't know that freedom is not a reward or a decoration that is celebrated with champagne. Nor yet a gift, a box of dainties designed to make you lick your chops. Oh, no! It's a chore, on the contrary, and a long-distance race, quite solitary and very exhausting . . . At the end of all freedom is a court sentence; that's why freedom is too heavy to bear, especially when you're down with a fever, or are distressed, or love nobody . . . For anyone who is alone, without God and without a master, the weight of days is dreadful. Hence, one must choose a master, God being out of style."[2]

There is always a place, therefore, for the dictator in this world. He does the people a favor by taking away their freedom and making everything simple according to arbitrary rules. Is this not what the masses want: To be rapped on the knuckles for breaking the rules of the game, to be made secure by religious rituals, not to live their lives but to have them lived for them? "Why have you come to disturb us," says the Grand Inquisitor to Christ. "You are destroying our traditions and our security; do you not see that people cannot bear to be free, and that despite all the talk to the contrary, men deep in their hearts do not want to be free?"

Behind the cynicism of the dictatorial creed there do lie the serious and unanswered questions: Where is the freedom of freedom? Where is the power to enable men to bear freedom? Where is the object that will destroy neither man nor freedom? Nietzsche was right in finding intolerable the god who made man into a pawn to be manipulated; "man could not bear that such a witness should live." But once that has been done and the emperor god has been removed from the scene, there are only two alternatives remaining: either the annihilation of meaning to life in the absurdity of an eternal return or else the free acceptance of human life in the daring risk of faith.

What has become clear in all this modern discussion is that freedom is the most desirable and yet most fearful thing about human life. Insofar as contemporary men recognize that they are called to freedom, it would seem that the gospel would be of pertinence. It claims to deal

[2] Albert Camus, *The Fall* (New York, 1956), p. 132 f.

with the hard facts of human freedom. Men have struggled
to reach their goal by following the precepts that seemed
to lead in that direction. The discouraging thing is that
men have not been able to observe their own precepts.
It is bad enough to be forced to act against one's will,
but what is insufferable for man is to find that he cannot
control himself, let alone the rest of the world.

To the collection of religious rites and ethical systems,
Christianity is not supposed to add merely one more answer.
The gospel calls for a certain kind of reversal in religion
and ethics. Man, says the gospel, cannot attain freedom by
his own effort. He cannot find it, buy it, make it or steal it;
but if only he can relax and accept it, all will be given in
abundance. Freedom is that good which is the least expensive, the most valuable and the closest ready at hand;
all man has to do is surrender. To receive a true and
perfected freedom he must be ready to let go of the freedom he now possesses. "He that will seek to save his
freedom will lose it; and he that loses his freedom for my
sake keeps it unto eternal life."

This terrible moment of letting go ought not to be
covered over. Man must surrender absolutely, subjecting
his life to God who will raise him up. So long as man
seeks his own freedom exclusively or primarily, he will
never find it. As soon as he ceases that search and begins
to seek the divine intention for the whole human community, then he is already freed. "The most tremendous
thing which has been granted to man is: the choice, freedom. And if you desire to save and preserve it there is only
one way: in the very same second, unconditionally and in
complete resignation to give it back to God, and yourself
with it. If the sight of what is granted to you tempts you,

and if you give way to the temptation and look with egoistic desire upon the freedom of choice, then you lose your freedom. And your punishment is: to go on in a kind of confusion priding yourself on having freedom of choice, but, woe upon you, that is your judgment: You have freedom of choice, you say, and still you have not chosen God. Then you will grow ill . . . you sigh that you have lost your freedom of choice—and your fault is only that you do not grieve deeply enough or you would find it again."[3]

Man has to open up to God and accept what may come from his hands. This standing open at the center ought to be considered the focus of all human activity. Every step toward truth and every act of love is a movement inward to or outward from the complete surrender to God. The impression should not be given, however, that once such a choice is made, then the battle is over. The Christian life is supposed to be the progressive conquest of liberty and the gradual growth of freedom. Man's life has to be lived out moment by moment in time. Freedom is to work outward through all the levels of human flesh even to the transformation of the universe. All creation is to have its share in the liberty which belongs to the children of God. Just as the flesh of Christ was transformed through painful endurance, so all flesh is brought to freedom in patient acceptance.

Man cannot dictate the growth of his own freedom and the transformation of his own flesh. He actually has little control over conditions of heredity and environment. He often cannot overcome what he would like to overcome; he

[3] Soren Kierkegaard, *The Journals of Kierkegaard* (New York, 1958), p. 189.

cannot immediately eliminate anything out of his life. His
exercise of freedom lies mainly in the meaning he gives
to the determinisms already present in his life. "To *will*
does not mean to be willful, but rather to gain gradually
the power of increased judgment and decision in the application of drive. Man must learn to will what can be, to
renounce as not worth willing what cannot be, and to
believe he willed what is inevitable."[4] The freedom of the
sons of God lies in the recognition and acceptance of this
finitude. In all this, what the gospel does is hold together
passionate willing and patient humility. Every triumph of
Spirit over flesh is partial until the parousia.

As with the first step, every growth of freedom is accomplished not by the force of self-attention but by man
making himself available and transparent to others. There
is an impulse to freedom from within, but it must be
directed by the outer call to freedom made by other human beings. At every stage, freedom is a gift from God,
but just for that reason it is a task for all the children
of God. The freedom of each man must be desired as part
of the movement toward freedom for all. Separated from
the communal march toward freedom, the individual is
almost certain to fall back into a self-glorifying concept of
freedom which is nothing but a self-seeking security. To
the degree that the Spirit has transformed mankind, men
can act by love rather than fear and the freedom of all is
enhanced. Conversely, to the degree that any man's freedom is violated, then the freedom of every man is lessened.

The last statement shows the inadequacy of any individualistic approach to freedom. John Stuart Mill's descrip-

[4] Erik Erikson, *Insight and Responsibility* (New York, 1964), p.
118.

tion of the problem is representative of this inadequate position bequeathed to us from another age: "The only freedom which deserves the name, is that of pursuing our own good in our own way, so long as we do not attempt to deprive others of theirs, or impede their efforts to obtain it."[5] The statement seems logical enough but it presents a misleading starting point. The contemporary world reveals only too clearly that it is impossible to let individuals do anything they please up to the point at which they conflict with others. Practically every action of every individual conflicts with someone else; and nobody is satisfied with the lines that somebody else draws. A policy of "not depriving others" or "not impeding their efforts" is a failure in responsibility. What is needed is positive action to increase other men's freedom.

The contemporary world must situate the question of freedom in a social or communal context. Freedom is not a limited good of the individual which he must restrict for the sake of others. Freedom is an absolute good to be limited by nothing beyond itself; but at the same time it is from the start the freedom of a community. Each person must discover that to be free is to be free for loving his people; to be free is to establish that kind of dependency on others which develops personality. When the individual begins to understand that his life is relational, he will see that the choice is not between God and himself nor himself and other men. He must affirm all of them together. He knows that there is some truth to the dictum that "the illusion of freedom is to do what I want; the reality of freedom is to want what God does." This is not the last

[5] Quoted in Herbert Muller, *Religion and Freedom in the Modern World* (Chicago, 1963), p. 4.

word, however. The Christian believes that if he digs deep enough he will find an identity between what he wants to do and what God does. What God wants is the truth for man and the truth is that man is bound to God and his neighbor. "I am the truth," Christ said, "and the truth shall set you free."

Insofar as the church is living the life of the Spirit, the church is the standard and the home of freedom in the world. The church prays for the Spirit that he may come and abide "transforming us into that living unity, in which the obedience of all is unceasingly revealing itself as the only freedom."[6] Because the church of time is still en route, a war must be waged for freedom even within the church. The weapons of that war are the weapons of freedom: wisdom, patience and unbounded charity. The war is not between individuals in the church; the line of battle runs through the middle of every human heart. No man can stand alone in this war trusting only to his own vision of truth and his own possession of freedom. The call to freedom is the call forward as part of the human community.

For the Christian church, therefore, freedom is not one of the virtues; it is the meaning of Christian life. Jesus Christ was that remarkable individual who, because he was free, was able to communicate freedom to all men. The freedom which is spoken of throughout the New Testament is not a psychological or metaphysical freedom; these are presupposed. But neither is freedom "in Christ" a kind of second story built upon "natural freedom." The freedom of Christ is meant to confirm and to protect all

[6] Alexander Schmemann, "Freedom in the Church," in *The WORD in History, op. cit.* p. 132.

freedom. In this way, all human freedom will tend to transcend itself and become more than human; if it does not, it will sink to something less than human.

The Christian faith is a gift held out to those who can take hold of it. Those who accept it should become free thereby, and those who accept it as religious ought to manifest this freedom in a striking way. Whatever else he is, the religious ought to be an example and a witness to the freedom that characterizes Christian faith. It is ironic and tragic that most people would think that the religious's vow of obedience makes him less free. If this were true, one would need no better reason for eliminating the vow of obedience. Actually, even as presently conceived, the vow of obedience is a means for situating individuals in a community life dedicated to freedom. The question should never be one of choosing between freedom and obedience, freedom and order. The issue always is how to increase freedom in a way that also fortifies authority, order and obedience to God. Although in principle there is no conflict between obedience and freedom, it would be dishonest to pretend that there were not difficult problems in working this out in practice.

One hears religious superiors complain that the young religious today are not so submissive as they used to be. "How," these superiors ask, "can a religious house function if it is staffed with young revolutionaries?" It is true that there are many young religious today whose chief characteristic is not submissiveness, but this is hardly to their discredit. Most of them are interested in working for the kingdom of God as grown up sons (and daughters) of God. Most of them are quite willing to listen, though they also like to speak. They are committed to obeying the commands of a superior, though they insist that a superior demonstrate at least minimal competence. They object to replacing reason and research with mechanical, unimaginative application of rules. In short, what they desire is to put to work the available human resources to do any job.

The different world view of these young people is beyond the comprehension of many people schooled in another mode of life. The only thing that many older people in religious life can conclude is that the houses of formation are no longer doing the job. "Why don't they teach these young people some obedience?" is a remark not infrequently heard. It is understandable that such a statement could be made, but the remark is not to the point at all. There is no conspiracy among novice directors nor is someone else in the assembly line at fault. A new world has burst through the boundaries of the old system. The young religious are the way they are mainly because they are young people living in America in the last third of the twentieth century.

The movement toward freedom and personal responsibility is spreading like wildfire throughout the world—on every continent, at every level of society, in every corner of the country and throughout every part of the church. Some people think that we are the worse for this emergence; they may well be right. The indubitable facts are: 1) that this change has occurred, 2) that the process is irreversible. Communication media can spread the desire and demand for freedom faster than can be reformed the social structures needed for freedom. It remains to be seen whether the human race can survive this transitional gap. In any case, suspicion of conspiracies to undermine authority is somewhat ludicrous against the background of the historical movement.

It would be incredibly naïve, therefore, for religious congregations to think that their problems are caused by their houses of formation. These houses, with all their inherent limitations, have been doing a creditable job in bridging the gap to the contemporary world. Instead of being blamed for causing disturbances, most of them deserve praise for preventing disturbances that would be calamitous. Often, however, other houses in the congregation are painfully slow in making changes that are desperately needed. If young religious, on entering a community, urge changes in liturgy or religion curricula, they are hardly to be scolded for stirring up trouble. What they are doing is making known what has happened and continues to happen in the contemporary church. The religious who has discovered what it means to live with the freedom of a son ought to have room in his life for making his own personal decisions, for making experiments with new approaches to his work, and for having a prayer life that is not threatened by numerous devotional practices. Each religious congregation is already faced with the choice (though some do not have a suspicion of it): either it is taking the gospel with its message of freedom as the rule for responsible adults, or else it is moving toward extinction.

There should be recalled here the distinction elaborated in chapter five between the task side of life and personal-community life. Insofar as the young religious participates in the bureaucratic structure of modern society, he has to learn to abide by the authority structure. He can work to change it, but he ought to fulfill the requirements of his job. If he refuses to be cooperative, he should, like anyone else, be fired. Because of the failure to distinguish the two aspects of life, arguments over the superior's orders and the young religious's obedience are seldom to the point. The rebellions are often misplaced and sometimes a school or hospital suffers the consequences of someone working out his freedom problem in the wrong place. Some religious would be more responsible in their jobs if they could live like mature adults in the personal side of life. When it comes to this community aspect, young religious do not appreciate benevolent rulers. They want participatory democracy, pure and simple. As already indicated, this demand is not only compatible with obedience to God and world but is today necessitated by it. In the past, the carry over of an institutional form of obedience into the religious community led to some people turning in on themselves and leading lonely lives in the community. Today the young do not stay around long enough to become gripers behind the back of the superior; they simply pick up and leave.

The freedom which an individual has within an institution is always inherently limited. Human institutions produce a multiplicity of goods and a breathing space for the individual. They also endanger the individual by casting him into a sea of anonymity and a surfeit of possibilities. There is no freedom for an individual unless the individual knows something worth doing, has the desire to do it, and has the strength to act on his desire. Many people would be willing to put up with the shortcomings of the institution they are in if they had the supporting strength of a personality nurtured in a strong nuclear community.

The religious congregation is supposed to be the place where such liberating communities exist. Here, one does not try to insert a little dialogue into the system. Dialogue is the principle of life for the personal community. Communality, freedom and dialogue are different ways of describing the same reality. The group is a supporting personal community if it lives by dialogue and if in it men are growing in freedom.

The word "dialogue" has unfortunately suffered a good deal of overuse and misuse in recent years. It has been confused with much talking about everything. At its worst it has been used as a tool to siphon off rebellious elements. Thus there have developed democratic processes to enforce authoritarian decisions. More often than not, the misuse is not cynically or even intentionally perpetrated. It is simply that dialogue cannot work at the community level unless it is trusted to be *the* life principle of the community. But this can occur only when there is a tight enough network of personal existence so that one multivoiced conversation is feasible.

It seems silly to point out the essentials of a conversation, but the fact is that many people do not engage in conversation. Superficially, something appears to be a conversation but actually it is several monologues. In a true conversation the following sequence is somehow operative: 1) a person speaks; 2) someone listens both to the words spoken and to what the speaker is trying to convey; 3) the listener answers to what has just been presented and frames his answer with anticipation of how the other will react; 4) the first interlocutor answers to what the second has just said, interpreting the remark within the total context now created. It sounds so simple, and yet many people avoid the process by not listening to what the other person is trying to say. People try to score points rather than really learn something and change their minds on the basis of the conversation. They try to lead the discussion to what they think is the right outcome. Instead of listening, they are engaged in trying to think of the next remark that they will make to defend their position.

The crucial difference in true dialogue or conversation is its open-ended character. "To be a responder in a conversation is to participate in something that is not all worked out beforehand. Indeed, if the participants in a conversation come to it with preconceived ideas about what the conclusion should be, the conversation will never really begin."[7] Dialogue is co-extensive with freedom; both consist not in choosing pre-patterned alternatives but in generating new alternatives. In this open-ended process of growth there is nothing arbitrary or whimsical. There is a movement toward the truth but in the way that human truth can be affirmed, namely, by confirming the other person in his search for the truth with us. Truth will come through dialogue if love, confidence and fidelity are the supports of the conversation.

The man who has begun to sense what St. Paul means by the freedom of a son knows that it will not be attained by doing away with law. Rather, freedom emerges with the finding of the law of dialogic love that makes a community. Those Christians who are learning what it means to live with such freedom are signs of faith in a world that finds any kind of belief difficult. A man may not know

[7] Robert Johann, "Authority and Responsibility," in *Freedom and Man* (New York, 1965), p. 146.

what he wants when he asks for freedom, but when he meets a man of freedom he cannot but begin to suspect what freedom does mean. Every increase of freedom brings the world closer to God through and with the freedom of Christ. Whether or not men realize it, the desire for freedom is the desire for God.

8. Women of the Church

The most important thing to be said of sisters is that they are women of the church. The words "women" and "church" are important, but so is the word "of." It has frequently been asked and it is still often asked: What is the role of women in the church? But that is the wrong question. Women are not in the church; they are the church—or at least half of it. In this chapter we would like to comment briefly on the changing image of womanhood particularly within the Christian church. Then we shall suggest ways in which the sister can be a representative and leader in bringing out this feminine side of the church's life.

We have claimed in chapter three that the great revolution in church and society remains almost unnoticed, that is, the change in understanding womanhood. The future of the church depends upon the rise of women to a status equal with though different from men. Never throughout its past has Christianity accorded equality to women simply because it has taken Christianity this long to emerge from its pagan background. For this reason it is more accurate to think of the present era not as the end of Christian history but as the beginning.

A new form of human consciousness has recently emerged among us. When the threshold was crossed is not agreed upon; whether technology is primarily a cause of the revolution or an effect is debatable. What is certain beyond doubt is the fact of the revolution. Other ages may have thought that they were in the midst of revolution. It is only this era which knows enough about the past to be certain that it is indeed different from every other era that has preceded it. This statement indicates what are the distinguishing marks of contemporaneity, namely, a future-oriented world and a society centered upon the interpersonal.

The world has never before lived with an awareness that the future would be decidedly different. We are not well prepared to live in a world creating its own future; perhaps by definition we cannot be prepared in detail. Schools and teachers are slowly beginning to grasp that they cannot transmit the knowledge which students will need in later life. The world in which the student will live not only does not exist but is almost beyond imagination. Not just the teachers of physics and mathematics but even teachers of theology cannot pass on the body of correct answers to known problems. Education can only strive to shape a style of thinking in people so that when they meet future problems they may bring to them a creative response.

Within the constantly accelerating movement of society, the community such as the family may seem hopelessly inadequate to cope with the situation. Paradoxically, however, it is destined to re-emerge at the center of any solution. The breaking open of man toward the future has revealed man to himself; he can see more clearly than ever that he is the being for whom "to be" is "to be with." Science and technology are the greatest threat to human community but also its greatest opportunity. Science has made possible on a world-wide scale the encountering of man with man. As we now face the future there is acute awareness of the place of the individual and the need to achieve a sense of community.

It is at this point that the feminine aspect of the revolution becomes central. What women now ask for, namely, independence, freedom and the right to personal fulfillment, have long been claimed by the male. What needs recognition is not only that men must allow these for women but also that man himself cannot seek his personal development except in relation to his feminine companion, who is not just his emotional fulfillment but a partner in the full sense. There are some Americans who like to pretend that the patriarchal society still exists, but in fact it died long ago in the places where it existed. If we can admit this fact and rejoice in it, we can get on with the building of human and participant communities in which decisions are made by equals for the freedom and love of all.

The church's function in this vortex of change is easy to discern though difficult to sustain. The church is to urge the world forward to its own best possibilities. She is to destroy the idols men build and to keep the future open for visionaries. She is supposed to be engaged in creating a community of love, though she cannot spell out clearly what that entails. This inadequacy is not so bad, however, for admitting that she does not already possess the answer is the first step toward her future. In the humble role of pressing forward alternatives, the church is not guaranteed that she will be successful according to any criteria of success which we use. It is not recorded that the prophets of Israel or Jesus of Nazareth were ever given testimonials of success.

No society gives approbation to its own prophets, those who in unpredictable ways force a society forward to its own destiny. It is not by chance that the prophets have most often arisen among the poor, the maimed and the underprivileged. Prophecy comes from those who hate the conditions of their society but love their society enough to believe that it is worth transforming. This love with hatred requires an intuitive and affective kind of knowledge, a pondering in the heart which the Bible attributes to Daniel, Jacob and Jeremiah as well as to the Virgin Mary. Rebellion with love is what is needed for prophets and it is most often found among women. We have never had the number of women prophets we need; if Christianity is to reveal the full range of human possibilities, it cannot go on with this deficiency.

In American life today, the determination of whether the community will look narcissistically inward or Christianly outward is largely determined by women. By unassuming but decisive ways, the woman chooses whether to build impermeable walls or to build a community without walls. We have clear evidence from the ghetto and the suburb that the American Catholic woman can react with the violent defensiveness of un-Christian attitudes. We also have become aware that it does not take many women with educational capabilities, dedicated charity and courageous convictions to turn the tide. This is the age for women redeemers. Fortunately, we do not need great numbers of them, but we cannot get along at all without a few of them.

In the movement to secure equality for women, the feminist movement outside the church is somewhat ambivalent. It was Nietzsche who said that one should not be turned away from a movement by its first advocates. Although some of the best known feminist writers seem caught in their personal problems, most of what they advocate is not only compatible with but supported by Christian theology. The underlying principle of feminist writing seems to be that the biological differences between men and women are of minor importance compared to social conditioning. There is an important Christian truth here which St. Paul pointed to when he said that "in Christ there is neither Greek nor barbarian, Jew nor gentile, male or female, but all are one" (Gal. 3:28). Nevertheless, while insisting on the fact that men and women are not different species of the human being, we must not reduce the polyphony of masculine and feminine into a dull monotony.

Our world is threatened by activism and by a desperate flight from dependence. The exercise of power over matter easily leads to an egocentric attitude combined with manipulative tendencies. There is need for a counterbalance of other attitudes which are somewhat ambiguously but not without justification called "feminine." Dependence, sensitiveness and receptivity are not found solely among women, but they are found predominantly there. It is by the manifestation of a truly human dependence and a contemplative attitude among women that men will be enabled to accept their own feminine qualities. This is not a peripheral matter for Christianity; it is Christianity which clearly reveals that dependence is at either end of human development: both in the unwilled world of passivity and in the peak acceptance of faith. Before God all men are feminine. It is possible but unlikely that men of the church can discover this truth in themselves and hold onto it by themselves. However, for the demonstration that waiting in hope is not cowardice, that contemplation in quiet is not laziness, that needing another human being is not weakness, this is where is needed that "somantic design that harbors an inner space" (Erikson).

The difficult task for those growing up today is the creation of a world in which artificial differences between human beings is phased out while the rich variety of individual persons is heightened. Any community turned in on itself has already begun to die. The most genuine love cannot live for long if nourished only by its own substance. Love must be placed at the service of that which transcends it; only in this way can it resist the attrition of time and habit. Christian faith is the prohibiting of stopping short and taking half of reality for the whole, of either settling permanently in a corner of reality or ranging about everywhere in vague, uncommitted fashion.

The sister is today moving into the position of mirroring human development by moving within many communities. Most sisters have by now had experiences of human community outside the convent. The occasions may have been ecumenical meetings, civil rights demonstrations or peace protests. Though small in numbers, the sisters have been a visible and effective part of such groupings. The experience of community outside the convent has been a dominating force for renewal within. In this process, sisters have become more convinced of a twofold truth, namely, that their primary work is people and that they cannot get on with this work of being for others without the support, strength and love of their own primary community.

A human community implies a degree of autonomy and self-governance which sisters have never possessed. Religious women have never had a voice in the policy making decisions of the church, especially in those decisions affecting their lives and the institutions they serve. This arrangement may not have been so bad in that up to the present it has kept sisters free from vested interests. This freedom has allowed them to move where those in high places have difficulty finding entrance, especially among minority groups and the poor. It must be said, nevertheless, that the incapacity to determine the direction of one's own life is becoming an intolerable situation. The young woman now being reared in America cannot abide by the governmental structure in the church for taking care of sisters. Major superiors in this country might make it one of their chief tasks to educate church officials on the nature of religious life in America and the characteristics of American women. It is only in this way that there can be implementation of the Council's injunction that the institutes themselves have the most important role in renewal.

In this matter of self-determination, it would be wrong to suggest that all the troubles come from ecclesiastical authorities. Sisters up until recently have been schooled in the acceptance of all directions from above as God's will. The passivity they have often shown in the face of stagnation is lamentable. Many situations exist because people tolerate them, for example, the unrevised parish liturgies in many parts of the country. There are diplomatic ways of initiating the process to change these situations, but they have been used too infrequently. Hopefully, the sisters' senates and parish councils now being formed will provide opportunities for developing future oriented programs.

The heterogeneity of sisters' communities presents an

obstacle to unified life in the community. At the same time this diversity affords the opportunity for a rich variety of works. Many middle-aged and older sisters feel threatened by the exuberance, mobility and casualness of the young. There is a danger that they will abdicate the opportunity for contact with outsiders to the young sister. If this should happen, innumerable contacts and much good would be excluded. Retired sisters, for example, could provide wisdom and counsel to senior citizen groups and over-fifty clubs in their neighborhoods. These sisters would be welcome visitors in nursing and convalescent homes. In hospitals, their presence among the critically ill would be a source of peace. During the day, while convents are unoccupied, the retired sister could be hostess for small groups who wish to come in and pray. Religious communities could provide for the stranger seeking comfort and rest. The essential note of a Christian community is that it excludes no person in need, recognizing with the rule of St. Benedict that "all strangers are to be received as Christ."

The position of the middle-aged sister is also crucial. There is great need in convents for bridgebuilders, people near enough to the young to understand and near enough to the old to explain. Those sisters between the ages of forty and sixty, who are old enough to have experienced the wisdom of the old and young enough to be fired by the idealism of the young, are the pivotal members of renewal movements. The withdrawal of any age segment from the task of building a better society would be destructive of the human community.

The most common way in which sisters have become involved in other communities has been in parishes. Sisters are more conscious today that they are present to serve the total parish. They have been appearing in the homes of parishioners and more often letting their own homes function as parish centers. The sisters' contribution is sometimes challenging (for example, in presentations of theology or sociology), sometimes reassuring (for example, communal recitation of the rosary), almost never boring. For sisters there has been a new dimension in these contacts. In the atmosphere of the family living room the sister finds herself more able to serve and to understand. Married laymen have also come to discover that the distance between themselves and sisters is less than they had assumed.

The trouble with this expanding of work commitments is that it adds further burdens to people whose lives may already be overloaded. The policy making people in sisters' congregations are rightly concerned about the fragmenting of time and energy in these new works. The answer lies not in curtailing developments but in cutting out some of the older commitments and observances. More positively, steps must be taken to create conditions that provide for privacy and leisure. The five day week, which has become a standard for the professional American worker, is unknown in the life of the sister. As more frequent outside activities become commonplace, members of local communities must serve one another in planning and living. Unnecessary activities (for example, counting collections, washing altar linens, waxing floors) must be resolutely curtailed.

In addition to this reduction of the work load, there has to be a genuine education in leisure. It would be a tragedy if sisters were to think that leisure is of no value or find it a source of guilt. Perhaps sisters should stop expecting so much of themselves and realize that they too need to be re-created. A problem arises in that people are re-created in diverse ways. Although general chapters have been instructed to promote the vitality of the members, it is impossible to dictate how an individual is to be re-created. For one person it is a movie, for another music, for another a good conversation, for another a game of tennis. The freedom to decide the nature of one's leisure is an inalienable right. Such freedom does not destroy a community; it is more likely that a relaxed and revived sister will bring more to her sisters at home. Before carrying out this plan, some kind of psychic readjustment may be necessary in the mind of the individual sister. The sister may be still trying to fulfill some iron work horse image that traditional piety created for her.

The increased involvement of sisters in ecumenical work preserves them from too much self-conscious reflection. The expanded personal horizon that has come from relationships with other Christians and Jews is one of the prerequisites of future unity. Sisters are involved in community interfaith projects and other social action. Their presence in Protestant (though not Jewish) seminaries has become fairly common. Their involvement on the secular campus, either in student organizations or as Newman personnel, is another token of engagement with the world. What must be honestly faced is the effect that participation in non-convent, non-church settings will have on the individual sister and the local community. It is unrealistic to suppose that there will ever again be a sister image to fit all sisters. The question is whether any single image is desirable. It would seem that each sister must mirror the pluralism of the age. Convents in the last third of this century will be characterized by ecumenism and pluralism or else they will fail to reflect the Incarnation for this age.

The fact that sisters have been involved in protests and demonstrations is well known. What is not always admitted is that the underlying principles of such activities, if carried to their conclusion, will radically change the operative concepts of religious life. If a sister is free to witness to her convictions in any way she deems appropriate, there is no telling what may happen. There might be, for example, a rediscovery of a ministry to prisons. Convent refectories have for many years been the setting for readings about Perpetua and Felicitas, Lucy and Cecilia. Congregations founded in the period of the French Revolution are not strangers to this tradition. Prisons have never been unfamiliar places to the most loyal followers of one who was a condemned criminal. In today's world such a ministry has great implications. Visiting the imprisoned is a work of mercy which the elderly sister might recall to some of the young sisters. In addition, however, education for the poor and disadvantaged will have to include those people whose relationship to society is damaged and insecure. This problem looms at least as large among women as among men.

The main outside relationships that the sister still has is contact with the clergy. On one end of the spectrum are the clergy who feel that sisters will set everything right, that is, restore the older piety; at the other end are those who conjecture that most heretics today are found in convents. In between these two poles there is a great variety of attitudes. There are bishops who have been surprised by the bold steps taken by sisters within their dioceses. These bishops now look forward with either fear or encouragement to sisters' senates being formed. There are understanding and articulate priests who champion from afar the cause of sisters. There are men of the church who are aware of the sisters as women and as partners; their masculinity is in no way threatened by the admission of these women to equal status with them. It is to these men that sisters must currently look for a revision of attitudes and legislation pertaining to sisterhoods.

A point of legislation that must at least be considered is the ordination of sisters. One of the most serious obstacles in many sisters' lives is their dependence on the priest for the Eucharist. The liturgy in convents, especially parish convents, is often frustrating. To engage in hours of mass preparation only to be passive spectators at a hurried mass borders on the intolerable. Sisters know that they can devise other services without the presence of a priest. Nevertheless, their lives are rooted in the church and the church is rooted in the Eucharist. The Eucharist is to be the church at her best. If sisters are to have the freedom to strive for that best, it seems reasonable to consider having a sister-in-community celebrate the Eucharist for the community.

This proposal would seem to have a validity to it, but the reaction it draws from priests is at best a grudging acceptance. That it will eventually occur seems likely; nothing succeeds like an idea whose time has arrived. It may be prepared for by those aspects of the ministry that sisters are engaged in today, namely, counseling, nursing, visiting the sick, working with addicts, helping unwed mothers, catechizing, giving preparation for sacraments and organizing welfare programs. The ordination of sisters would help to preserve a community prayer life. The support provided by a rich liturgical life is of the greatest importance in meeting the problems that beset the sister today: the questioning of her relevance, the establishing of priorities and the meaning of celibacy. Community is the strongest factor in the favor of sisters; the Eucharist of the community is at the deepest level the base of operations.

Much of the present chapter deals with a future that does not yet exist. Yet this future is much closer to existence than we generally suppose and far more real than the dead past which is used as an argument against it. It is a future that must be created by individuals. There will never come a time when it will be easy not to be dragged down by the commonness of things to which we are tempted to adjust our vision. How the details are to be worked out in a person's life can only be determined by that person one step at a time. Feminist writing often speaks of a life plan that is to be rather rigidly maintained. Christianity speaks instead of a vocation for each person which implies a constantly changing dialogue of give and take, growth and adjustment, fidelity and love. In the contemporary search for new ways of life, the sister stands in an excellent position to demonstrate the variations possible in being human, Christian and feminine.

9. Christian Fraternities

There is a presumption throughout this book that will appear strange to many people, namely, that the way for a man to be in a celibate group is to be a brother. It cannot be denied that in church documents and in the public mind this is not the accepted position. Nowhere is this more evident than in the very places that canon law or Vatican II speaks of the "non-clerical male religious." Definitions are cast in reference to the clerical as if clerical and religious were almost synonymous. So strong is this public image that it is almost hopeless to stand against it. Nevertheless, the theme of this chapter is that the future of religious life depends upon the recovery of the brotherhood or fraternity as the model of the life.

A certain bias in the presentation of this idea is frankly admitted. One of the authors belongs to a "non-clerical male religious congregation" and this undoubtedly shades the opinions expressed. It would be unfortunate, however, if this essay were looked upon as an anti-clerical tract or as a defense of the vested interests of existing brothers' congregations. The present essay is not so much an advocacy of non-clerical congregations as an assertion of the necessity of brotherhood as the foundation of the congregation. If some men are ordained as priests, they should not have to stop being brothers.

The present schizophrenia finds some groups with more priests than they know what to do with (hence the strange

135

performance called concelebration) and other groups with no priests at all (hence the man who is supposed to serve the community is necessarily excluded from the community). Anyone with a logical mind must boggle at this confused arrangement. It would be tempting, though naïvely unrealistic, to suggest that everyone realign in a more sensible pattern. The history of this problem is very illuminative of a great deal of the struggle for a Christian life. This chapter is not so much on the brother as on the meaning of priesthood and lay life as these can be understood by an understanding of Christian fraternity.

We would underline this last point, namely, that this is not the chapter on brothers as if the other eleven chapters were not. The *book* presents the program for brotherhoods and sisterhoods. In the latter part of the chapter there are some specific suggestions for congregations of brothers, but only in the nature of showing what existing brotherhoods might do to lead the way toward the ideal presented in this book. Our main concern here is the relation of brotherhood to priesthood and celibate brotherhood to lay life. The result of this approach should be an increase in the understanding of all of them rather than an attempt to exalt one at the expense of another. Occasionally, an article on brothers appears (usually written by a priest) maintaining that brothers should be given more status and treated as the equal of clerics. With all due respect for the suggestion, many brothers react with the same gratitude as negroes who are told that they are going to be given equal status in white society. It is not equality that people are demanding today, it is a new kind of society. The time for paternalistic gestures is past. For example, if someone thinks that the brother should be grateful for being offered minor orders in replacement for being mass server, then that man understands little of the temper of today's society. A better case in point is the introduction of a modified breviary into brothers' congregations. Theoretically, such a move is not wrong insofar as the office (or at least part of it) should be the prayer of the whole church. The fact is, however, that this element has for so long been a clerical affair that unless a correction is made in the nature and practice of a liturgical office, then introducing it into the brother's community may just give the impression of clericalization.

The example points up the need for reunderstanding church and ministry. To build celibate fraternities it will be insufficient to say nice things about brothers or patch up existing brotherhoods. There will have to be a bigger movement involving all segments of the church. One of the most fascinating developments in Protestantism has been the rediscovery of the fraternity as an authentic element of the church. The community at Taizé in France is the most famous of these groups, though there are other similar groups that have begun to develop. If Protestants can re-establish this fraternity, then Catholics would presumably be in a better position to do so, since the idea has never been entirely lost in Roman Catholicism.

The mysteriousness of the brother's existence, instead of destroying its significance, constitutes its importance. The uncertainty of explanation even among brothers themselves has been fortunate because the existence of the fact has continued to pose to the whole church the question of vocation. The value of the brother's life has been and will be that it prevents a polarization of the church into laity and clergy. To prevent this split is no mean feat.

There are, of course, sisters to do the job; their choice in life is also a mystery to many people. But the sister does not pose the same kind of mystery because people assume that they know why sisters are not priests. They presume that if you wish to work officially in the church but you are a woman, then obviously you cannot be a priest but only the correlative, namely, a sister. The same explanation does not work for a brother. It is often said to brothers: "Why did you become a brother? Why didn't you go all the way and become a priest?" This is a sad question and not just because it is an insulting one. It is sad because it shows on the one hand so little appreciation of the priesthood, but more shockingly it shows no appreciation of the laity. For the lay questioner in asking this is not so much condemning the brother for going half way as depreciating himself for not going any of the way.

The tendency for many centuries has been to divide the church into two kinds of life: the clergy who are practically identified with church and the laity who are at worst outside the church, or more commonly under the church or at best in the church. This conception of church does a great disservice first of all to the clergy. Priesthood is not only not the only state of life in the church; it is not a state at all. Priesthood is a way of living in and serving a community. It is not a way of life that should be set over against the life of the laity. The isolation of priesthood in this way is not helpful to the life of the priest or the effectiveness of his ministry.

In addition, the clergy-laity dichotomy shows an even worse misunderstanding of the laity. Thinking and language in church circles give the impression that the laymen do not really constitute the church. Of course, there has been copious writing of late on the "layman's aposto-late"; but phrases like "people of God" strewn everywhere do not overcome the long standing difficulty. All the theo-logical definitions have done very little to change the bias that there are two kinds of Christians: clergy and laity, the first who belong and the second who hang on.

The brother, instead of being a peculiar aberration be-tween clergy and laity, is a key to revealing the inadequacy of both conceptions. Harvey Cox makes reference to the Little Brothers of Jesus and their promise not to use the name Jesus until they are asked why they are there. Cox goes on to reflect that modern man may be asking the question of salvation when he puts to us the question: What are you doing here?[1] If the brother's life is a puzzle to many people, this may be to its favor in opening up the strange vocation of being a Christian. We look first to the relationship to priesthood and then to the question of the laity.

The celibate communities arose in the church with no special connection to priesthood or hierarchy. After Bene-dict, the monastic way of life became a dominating form for those trying to live the Christian gospel. A few men would be ordained in the monastery to serve the obvious priestly need of this kind of community. The abbot of the monastery could be a layman even if there were a bishop in the monastery. To be a monk was to join the brother-hood in a community sharing of life.

Early in the Middle Ages, for reasons not entirely clear, there began a strong movement to ordain all the monks as priests. This blurred the line of distinction between the

[1] *God's Revolution and Man's Responsibility* (Valley Forge, 1965), pp. 106–108.

monastic life and that of the canons regular, parish clergy who had come together to form communities. As the Middle Ages progressed, priesthood became thought of as a special status with a dignity that a man should aspire to. The consequence of this was the belief that one hundred masses in the monastery would be more fruitful than one minister serving his ninety-nine brothers. The danger that already existed of having one Christianity for the elite and one for the ignorant masses was further exaggerated. For within the orders there now developed a split between the priestly choir monk and the brother who did not have the aspiration to do other than manual work. To this day the problems of the lay brother in the clerical order remain quite different from those of the brother in the modern congregation.

There have been repeated attempts in history to re-establish the sense of lay fraternity. St. Francis and his friars constituted only one of many lay groups that arose in the twelfth and early thirteenth centuries. Most of them became heretical groups and this led the official church to insist that new groups take over one of the approved rules of life. This did not stop the growth of other forms of life in the later Middle Ages. The Brethren of the Common Life was one such group that included both clerical and non-clerical, married and celibate members. This group did much in the line of preaching and teaching and writing on spirituality. They were severe in their criticism of the religious orders of the time, although they did not deny the validity of the monastic life itself. Among women, the attempt to create a new kind of apostolic venture with the Ursulines was exciting but short-lived. The sixteenth-century church was wary of letting women out from behind their perpetual enclosures.

At the beginning of modern times, other movements did have more success among men. The most famous of these was the founding of the Jesuits, who were allowed to make some break with the monastic pattern. Taking up the lead of the Theatines, they conceived of new forms of community life, doing priestly work in a tightly organized system. With the same apostolic orientation, John Baptist De La Salle began a group of laymen in seventeenth-century France. They were to engage in education, particularly in running schools for the poor. De La Salle explicitly prevented any of his men from becoming priests and built into their rule some precautions against their moving in that direction. Thus his men were to study and teach in the vernacular, an innovation of no small importance. De La Salle had intended to have a priest superior after himself, but the sudden death of the first man chosen made De La Salle change his mind. From a logical point of view, the exclusion of priests was an extreme stand to take, but it was perhaps the best alternative he had. De La Salle recognized the need for someone to do this work and he wanted a trained team of men who would be at the immediate call of neither wife nor bishop.

It would be unfair to be too critical of the limitations inherent to the new fraternity. It was less the fault of De La Salle than some unimaginative men after him that the movement did not become more prominent. The modern congregation of brothers, like other lay movements, has been, if not a complete failure, not a rousing success. Looking back from the comfortable vantage point of the present, one can speculate on what might have happened if the brothers had been able to remain as spearhead of a lay movement in Catholicism.

The limitation that De La Salle had to work with was that the models available to him were severely limited. It was difficult enough to get going at all in the seventeenth century without also breaking totally from the monastic ideal. The essence of his rule was very simple, namely, that his men should have faith and zeal while taking direction from the scriptures. De La Salle, like all innovators, was unavoidably a man of his time with its strengths and weaknesses. His rule could not avoid reflecting both the monastic pattern he was extricating himself from and the particular needs of the men who came to live with him. As repeatedly happens in history, the original pattern gets turned into a rigid and static way of life. The genius of the innovating founder is swallowed up in the cloying remnants of peripheral accretions. One does not have to possess a long memory to recall the painful death agony of seventeenth-century French spirituality and fourteenth-century *devotio moderna*.

If the first apostolic congregations can be excused for not breaking with the monastic form, it is more difficult to understand the succeeding brotherhoods. Most of the larger brotherhoods now existing were founded in nineteenth-century France in the wake of the French revolution. For the most part, they took over the highly structured common life pattern that De La Salle had used. The fault still lay in the official stance of the church which let the congregation exist only as a lesser form of the ancient orders. The ideal was still the solemn vows of the monastic tradition, though the church allowed existence to the congregation with its simple vows.

The so-called secular institutes of the twentieth century could have been a continuation of the movement stretching back at least to the twelfth century. In some ways the secular institute has accomplished its mission of posing a new option for this age. Unfortunately, however, the secular institute has itself been tempted to take over monastic structures and devotions. In the minds of many people, the secular institute would be a lesser form of religious life, presumably for those who want a little religion but do not want to go all the way. The nod of official approbation is supposedly a help to its growth. It remains to be seen, however, whether the new forms of Christian fraternity will spring from present secular institutes.

One thing seems certain at present. Neither secular institutes nor existing brotherhoods have any future in clinging to monastic or clerical remnants. For example, the wearing of a religious habit in all the brothers' congregations has been particularly unfortunate. We have already dealt with this question as a consequence of the theology of the secular. Here we would add that it is more important for the brother than the sister to get rid of the religious habit. The sister is not mistaken for being something other than a sister. But in the public mind, the long black dress on a man is unavoidably the clerical sign. In street dress, most brothers broke from the Roman collar only to adopt some hybrid. Their half revolution put them into a category of something more than a seminarian and something less than a curate.

We said that De La Salle had to exclude priests from his brotherhood largely because of the misunderstanding of priesthood. Yet in doing this he did create something that speaks obliquely of priesthood. One should not choose to become a priest because he wants an exalted state in the church. Priesthood is a way of serving one's brethren. This can be carried out within the religious life or in other lay communities. Priesthood is separable from and combinable with both states of life. The existence of the brother is living testimony that men do not choose priesthood as a higher state of life, nor do men choose lay life as a lower state. The question is not one of high and low perfection at all. The life of a Christian can be manifested in a multiplicity of forms that are of value to church and society. The Christian life is not a hierarchy of perfections but a life that is multidimensional and polyphonous; a variety of shapes, sizes, colors, forms and purposes.

There is in the Council declaration on religious life a single sentence to the effect that non-clerical congregations might consider ordaining some of their men. At the beginning of the international chapter of De La Salle's group in 1966 there seemed to be some sentiment for introducing the priesthood. The great majority of the men (and Americans in particular) rejected the idea. The main objection to it lay in the fact that the strongest support for the move came from countries where it was believed that this would raise the status of brothers. To American brothers this seemed the worst possible reason for introducing priesthood into the congregation. It would seem to assent to what we have said must be clearly excluded, namely, that the church consists of first class clerics and second class laymen.

One could speculate, nevertheless, on the possibility of such a move. It might be one of the ways in the future to clarify the meaning of priesthood. The ordination of a few men in non-clerical congregations could be a demon-

stration of priesthood that is difficult to carry out elsewhere. Perhaps there is an enterprising bishop who would
be ready to do it now. All he would have to do is drop in
some morning and ordain Brother Smith, not changing his
name, his clothing, his state of life, and so forth. When
the brother dies, they can put in his obituary that he was
a teacher and writer and that among other things he
ministered at the Eucharist; that is, Brother Smith was a
priest. Even the posing of this in a hypothetical way helps
to illuminate the relation of priesthood to a man's life.
A man would not have to cease to be a brother to become
a priest. More importantly, men do not now cease to be
brothers in the wider community when they become
priests.

There already exist modern congregations that have
priests among their brothers. The maintenance of unity
in these groups has been difficult, but a few of them have
survived to the present. They have tried to keep a real
equality of clerical and non-clerical members. It is puzzling and ironic that these groups still change the way a
man dresses or the term by which he is addressed when he
becomes ordained. Of such small things are walls of segregation made. If these congregations would get over this
nervousness they would be in an excellent position to
demonstrate quickly that all men are brothers though
some are also priests. In other orders where the level of
reform is at the stage of letting the brothers use the
priests' recreation room, one wonders whether it is too
late to even attempt a recovery.

Some supporters of brotherhoods object to the fact that
clerical orders often call their seminarians "brother." This
is given as indication of the confusion between priesthood

and religious life, giving rise to the perennial question for the religious brother: "Aren't you ordained *yet?*" There is some truth to there being a confusion in the language, but the solution of not calling seminarians "brothers" would not seem to be the logical one. It would seem more sensible if they did not stop being called "brothers" even after they are ordained. In a society in which one of the chief characteristics is anti-paternalism, one can hardly think of a worse title for churchmen than "father." It is unfortunate that the American priest picked up the title rather late but became thoroughly identified with it. As a mode of address, we are not advocating anyone being called "brother"; we are suggesting that the identity of the celibate group could be specified as fraternity or brotherhood. In addressing the person it would seem best to follow the customs of our society. In America, a man is called "John," "Joe," and so forth by his friends; he is formally addressed as Mr. Smith or Mr. Jones. It is not a matter of insignificance how an adult is spoken to. Any negro who has had his first name overused or any middle aged woman who is referred to in an office as "the girl" understands the point we are making.

Present brotherhoods represent an infinitesimal part of church population. It is doubtful whether they are equipped to carry out the leadership role; however, this is not because of their size. The essential thing everywhere in the world today is not number but the right time and the right place and the right ideal. The fact that brotherhoods are practically ignored in church legislation is probably not to their disadvantage. Although the legal structure must eventually be transformed in order to be a help, one must admit that for the moment it is mostly a hindrance. The man in the non-clerical congregation has none of the entanglements of clerical regulations, has more protection than the individual layman, and as a man (regretably or not, this is still true) has more power in society than a sister. This outline of advantages may seem to be naïve given the present influence of brotherhoods. Yet the possibility of a breakthrough to new life is there if the spark of leadership emerges. In a church rapidly becoming declericalized but not yet laicized, brotherhoods stand in a critical position as a bridge to the new world. It is their job to join hands with the "emerging layman" who has little organization to back him. Time is running out, however, for brotherhoods to divest themselves of semi-clerical appearance and become part of this secular age. This joining may be their death knell, but there are lots of less glorious ways of dying.

The correlative of the sisterhood is the brotherhood. It is important that sisters be clear on this point and understand the significance of re-establishing religious life for men as Christian fraternities. Many people mistakenly think that the nun is a kind of woman priest doing the work of the bishop. A properly autonomous life for a sister would be more clearly needed and more easily established if the brotherhood existed with some evident force. If and when the celibacy option for priests becomes effective, then the celibacy issue for the first time will become clear, that is, as a possible life style for brothers and sisters. Some people suspect that when priests are allowed to marry no one will wish to be a brother. That may indeed be true, but if so, it would seem to be saying that sisterhoods are already doomed. If it is true that there is something lacking in a man making it in celibate life as a brother, it would have to be asked whether the same is not true of women being sisters. Some people seem to think that sisters are clamoring to be ordained and that they would have their lives fulfilled if they could become priests. This assumption is a little silly, if not insulting. That brotherhoods and sisterhoods must have their own ordained ministers is a situation that must surely come to pass. But the survival, reform and fulfillment of the celibate teams is a question of the possibility of life as brotherhoods and sisterhoods. An order of men that thinks it will survive because of its clerical character is in for a rude shock. This is not meant as a slur upon orders in which all of the men are ordained for a work which is a priestly one. We are simply asserting that the refounding of religious life as a federation of local fraternities is the common task of clerical and non-clerical groups.

One thing in the favor of existing brotherhoods is that they have had to rely on their own solidarity. If they move forward, this will be a point of strength, though if they begin disintegrating, it will be a weakness. They are less overladen than clerics with confusion about authority channels and jurisdiction. If they chose to do it, brotherhoods could move very quickly into the compact teams which are autonomous at their own level. For initiating novel approaches to religious education, a teaching congregation of brothers would be in a very strong position. Most of the religious education of the future will not be done by an army of teachers in an enormous school system. The future seems to lie with informal programs for dealing with youth and theology centers for reaching adults. The great need will be not for large numbers of people to fill grade levels but for small teams of skilled men who have a sense of community, theology and education. If teaching congregations of brothers would immediately commit men to solid theological training, they could in a short time lead the lay movement in theology and religious education.

This suggestion should not be understood to mean that the specific work of brotherhoods is catechetics. The history of the catechetical movement is largely one of trying to save the catechetical mission of the church from catechetical experts. That is, if religious education is going to be tried at all, it must be given a broad human base. It requires men with both theological and non-theological learning drawing on wide educational experience. Catholic and Protestant Sunday schools notwithstanding, it is no job for people with a textbook, a spare hour and a certificate. Precisely to make a contribution to religious education, brotherhoods need men who are trained as psychologists, historians, linguists and so forth. In contact with their brothers and in informal ways with outsiders, they will contribute to the only kind of religious education that has a future in the Catholic church, namely, reaching adults with a meaningful life and an intelligible theology.

The broader aspect of the life of brothers would be involvement in both church sponsored and public supported education. The Catholic school, particularly in the city, will probably continue to exist. Brotherhoods are already making a sizable contribution there, but with increased flexibility they could become even more effective. Moreover, they are in a good position to move into those public schools where the need is urgent and other teachers feel the lack of a common support. Public officials may be wary of hiring priests, since they think they know what priests are. The brother is just enough unknown to move unostentatiously into public education.

These several kinds of work would enrich the community existence of the Christian fraternity. There is a feeling in some brotherhoods that their unity demands that they all work in the same institutions. This may have been true in the past, but this is not where the future lies. It is true that there would have to be some common bond to their works. But to have men working in public schools, Catholic schools and adult catechetical centers would provide plenty of common interest. A community in which the common topics of interest are things like the school football team is hardly enriching to the lives of adults. The commitment of a community to a single institution can unfortunately produce not a rich unity of diverse lives but a suffocating conformity of limited interests.

For the existing brothers to be a source of help to lay life, they do not have to do anything very extraordinary. In fact, they would best not try to do anything extraordinary if they do not have extraordinary people. Their job is to be with the layman showing by their persons that they understand faith and zeal. The "public witness" can come and will come later, if brotherhoods exist. They may never find out if they exist unless they give up the props shoring up the present institutions. The brotherhoods could give evidence that there is no need for a negation of any values in the life of the laity. The vows are still misunderstood as some kind of heroic sacrifice to perfect the individuals. The brother could show that the essence of the Christian life is not poverty, chastity and obedience but charity. The brother enters a community in order that this community may be a sign of joy and brotherly love among men.

Love, freedom, hope and joy are meant for all Christians as ideals to undergird every striving and as forces to affect every political structure. These ideals get clouded over with legalism and formality unless there are continual demonstrations of the ideals in their simplicity. The religious life is supposed to be a life according to the more simple style of the gospel. The church can then point to these communities as examples of her life. These individuals are not holier nor are they removed from the failings that belong to all men. Rather, it is here that one has the structure for taking a risk with human freedom because the community is set up to bear with human failure.

Christianity is to be a union of free men who work for an increase of love among all. The whole of Christianity cannot function as a community, dispersed as it is through the world. Within the Christian church, therefore, there have to be small communities that mirror this communal love. The church does it primarily through the family in the love between father and mother that shines forth in the child. But the family has its own structure and it is even more restricted in its function than in earlier eras. All possibilities are not exhausted by the family. Christianity, to complement the family, has the strange phenomenon of religious life. Although the brothers in one part of life will be professional and at home in secular society, their community existence will be dictated by the simple demands of the gospel. There are many places in the world where the example of men who can live together without going at each other's throats would be of inestimatable value for making divine love and human love credible once more.

The brother thus commits his life to God according to a way of life in the church. Precisely because the man is dedicated to such a life there is no need to dictate every moment of his existence by a series of rules. Here is where one must trust people to make their own decisions according to the goals of the community and the good of the members. The law that governs the community is the law that is inherent to communal love. The brotherhood ought simply to express in striking form values already present in lay life. If someone objects that this is not what religious congregations provide, he may be right. It is time for the celibate fraternities to produce or close down. The obedience demanded today is the going forward to a new form of brotherhood as the foundation of celibate life. "For standing still is disobedience for Brothers advancing toward Christ."[2]

[2] Rule of Taizé, as quoted in John Heijke, *Renewal of Religious Life Taizé* (Pittsburgh, 1967), p. 89.

10. Doing Away with Poverty

With the exception of religious orders, everyone else in the modern world seems intent upon doing away with poverty. Nothing so betrays the irrelevancy of religious life as the typical chapter on "How to Practice the Virtue of Poverty." The thesis of this essay is that a vow of poverty is useless and a virtue of poverty is illusory. The one main thing to be said about poverty is that it is a social evil which must be cured as quickly and as completely as possible.

It will no doubt be objected that there is an "evangelical poverty" that is different from the deprivation of material goods. Writers on religious life have always pointed out the poverty of spirit that Christ praised in the beatitudes. It is added that this spirit will best be maintained if the religious does not have many luxuries. It is all right to be comfortable, but one should not be too comfortable.

The trouble with even the best of these essays is that they ring hollow. They do not sound very convincing to the religious themselves and they sound positively dishonest to many people outside religious life. As has been true of several other words discussed in this book, the word "poverty" in one meaning says too much and in another meaning says too little. Because consideration starts from too narrow a base, the truly profound meaning that the word "poverty" could have is not penetrated. On the other hand, the more obvious meaning of "poverty" is pretentiously spoken of as if religious life were a particularly good example of it.

The word "poverty" is too sensitive a word to be lightly used today. Theoretically, there is no reason why people in religious life could not claim a certain poverty. We shall insist, in fact, that there is a poverty that pertains to all men. But the currency of the language in religious congregations has been devalued through long abuse. If it were possible, religious would do best to put a moratorium for a few decades on the use of the word "poverty" in reference to themselves. If they must talk of poverty, let them look out at the poor human race and ask themselves how they can aid the rest of mankind in its struggle to eradicate poverty and wretchedness. The "vow of poverty," in any case, ought to be done away with. We have spoken already of the meaninglessness of taking three or more vows. Whether or not some formal promise should be retained, the taking of a series of vows, each supposedly having an object, is not only useless but misleading. It was the attempt to conjure up some virtuous thing called "poverty" that has largely been responsible for the debasement of language in this area.

Since we are so pessimistic about the language and about the possibility of redefinition, it may seem strange that we broach the topic at all. It must be admitted that the whole chapter is likely to be self-defeating, for we are protesting loudly that religious should not protest at all on the subject. Aware of this dilemma and danger, we must nevertheless deal with this topic because the financial issue is absolutely crucial to the whole matter at hand. We must speak of the notion of poverty in religious life if only to destroy it. More to the point, we must assert the need to shift the whole financial base of the operation.

Questions of money are not often discussed in public by the church, presumably so that men's minds can be more preoccupied with less mundane affairs. Nevertheless, some people in religious life are concerned with almost nothing else than how to pay the bills. They would be quite happy, no doubt, if the congregations let go of their medieval remnants of poverty and put the operation on some stable financial footing. The only ones who might not like the change would be administrators of the institutions that have been able to exist because of the supply of cheap labor. One can sympathize with their problems, but their supply is drying up anyway. To begin paying people for what their services are worth would probably be the death of some Catholic institutions, but it would certainly be the resurrection of others. By being considered as something other than low cost help, the celibate groups might find better reasons for their existence. At least they would be forced to look. As we have candidly admitted with all these suggestions, the implementation of this proposal could mean the dissolution of the whole life. Just as with the religious habit, this is a question with tremendous implications. Once people acquire economic responsibility, they begin to get all sorts of other ideas.

In this whole consideration, there is no disparagement of the sisters who have faithfully served in the past. Their services often could be performed without expensive training and for an important need of the time. But the fact today is that no one is willing to justify his life by being considered cheap labor. If religious congregations cannot exist except by being the supplier of inexpensive labor, then it is perhaps better that they do dissolve.

Before considering some of the moves that religious might make to reduce poverty in the world, it will be well to consider the strand of biblical tradition that gradually became distorted in religious life. That there is a very central place in scripture for the poor of the Lord is well known. The point we would stress is that scripture reveals the essential poverty of being man. Man is called to be man and thereby to recognize that his possessions are not his own. The Bible conveys this fact not by romanticizing about poverty but by showing that God has taken to himself in a particular way the poor, the suffering, the downtrodden and the dispossessed. It is not that these people are better than everyone else. Rather, says the prophet to the poor people, God shows his great mercy and his tender love that he can choose *even* you.

Here is that center of the tradition that we have previously considered from several other angles. God, the faithful one, wishes simply to let man be man. But man keeps refusing to affirm the whole world and the whole human family. The result, as we pointed out in chapter four, is that the acceptance of the secular is not quite so easy as it may appear to the rational minded secularist. Man's reason is a gift never to be put aside, but reason is not ultimately judge of the universe. Just when man seems to have figured out everything for himself, he is challenged by some inexplicable phenomenon at the periphery of his vision. If he looks closely enough, he may find that the chosen experience is not peripheral at all but represents a severe challenge to the rest of his experience. In modern fiction, Flannery O'Connor has caught this spirit in the grotesque characters found in her short stories. Through these characters, without being expected and without being desired, there comes a shattering blow to human pretentiousness.

There is no confusion of values in this biblical tradition. Life is better than death, health is preferable to sickness, richness is better than poverty. But what is realistically faced is that poverty, suffering and death are facts of human life. Men try to pretend that they are minor facts and can generally be forgotten. However, the facts never go away; they nag continuously. Some day they must be faced so that man's attitude to God, his neighbor and himself may be tested against them. Is it possible to accept life as a gift from God when life leads only to suffering and death? Only if a God of love can be revealed even in suffering and death. Can a God rich in beauty be believed in if some men lie in poverty and squalor? Only if God is revealed even in the poor and downtrodden.

One does not have to love poverty, but one should go out to the unloved poor. One certainly does not have to contrive methods of inflicting suffering on oneself; there will be more than enough in the course of things as one tries to cure poverty. "To agree that Christian suffering is voluntary does not mean that the Gospel bids us run in search of self-torment; instead, suffering is encountered and accepted in connection with fidelity to aims that we whole-heartedly espouse. As Christians we believe that pain is an evil, all other things being equal; and we seek to reduce it in our lives as well as in the lives of others."[1] At times we may not be able to do anything except be

[1] Roberts, *op. cit.,* p. 140.

there with those who are poor or sick. When it is possible, however, we must use the tools available to cure sickness and poverty.

The test of the whole mission of the church is her concern for the deprived, the "useless" people. We are called to love all of our brothers and not to close out judgment on the human race. But whereas we are quite adept at accepting the clean, virtuous and well behaved, we are frightened by the unkempt stranger in the shadows of our world. If there is no concern for the poor outcast, then the question the church must ask is whether she has lost her sense of how every man stands poor and naked before his creator. If the poor are broken or expelled by the church, then the church has perhaps lost all sense of her mission to mankind: "To bind up the broken hearted, to proclaim liberty to the prisoners, to proclaim the year of the Lord's favor" (Is. 61:1–2).

Throughout the early centuries of Christianity the church attracted to herself many of the urban poor who were waiting for a message of hope. Who could object to a word of comfort to those who had to live in misery? Rich men who wished to dramatize their concern with the gospel could give away their wealth and lead a simple life. Thus when men entered the monasteries they renounced their possessions to share all things in common. In this way, there was continued under another form the mutuality of concern and goods which is recounted of the whole church in the Acts of the Apostles. There was guaranteed for the monk a minimum security so that he could be attentive to divine contemplation.

In most centuries the simple monastic life has provided a sharp contrast to the society about it. Presumably, in

some new form it can continue to offer a refreshing difference in the twentieth century. In the Middle Ages, variations in life form had already developed away from
monasticism. The mendicant orders challenged their society by protest in the form of begging. The luxury of
being comfortable in one's possessions has needed challenge in every century. The monasteries, however, and
eventually even the mendicant orders, were not without
their own dangers in combining the ascetical minimalness
of the individual with the wealth of the institution. Rein-
hold Niebuhr has warned us in recent times of the tendency of individual vices to be transposed into collective
virtues. Freeing the individual from concern with his own
economic position does not in itself guarantee the elimina-
tion of greed, pride and power politics. The only real
protection against the growth of such vices under guise
of gospel simplicity is in the whole community looking
out beyond itself to those who are most in need.

This was the greatness of the apostolic congregations
that arose at the beginning of modern times. Without
negating the continuing validity of the monastic ideal, they
jumped into the political-social-economic fray that was
giving birth to modernity. It took a while to convince
church officials that this, too, was a legitimate way for
celibate men to witness to the coming of the kingdom.
It has taken much longer to make the same point in regard
to women.

With the Jesuits, the modern style congregation came
into existence. Much of what had characterized the monasteries (for example, the divine office in common) was
recognized as inappropriate. The new task demanded
new forms of community life. Although the principle was

accepted, the full implications of it have never quite become clear. All kinds of remnants of the monastery, intended to create the atmosphere of calm and unchanging serenity, crept unexamined into the life of the new congregations. The alliance has always been a somewhat uneasy one, but the grasp of the older elements was tenacious. One need only go over the hundred odd little touches that characterized the *horarium* in all the congregations (not to mention the existence of a *horarium*).

Nowhere was this confusion greater nor the effect more deleterious than in the rhetoric of poverty. The attempt to adapt the medieval concept to these new congregations was a hopeless endeavor from the start. This is not to say that the congregations did not produce great numbers of good and holy men; they did. But the vow of poverty was never much of a help to the project and has increasingly become a hindrance. The monk in an earlier era had protested by the means available to him against the misuse of wealth. The modern congregation arose precisely because new means were becoming available in the emerging world. "Since the rise of industry . . . and the establishment of large enterprises the meaning of riches has undergone a drastic change. Gone is the primary implication of a life filled with excessive pleasures and of profits accruing solely to the owners' capital. Today ownership and capital are primarily a social-productive factor. Capital now means prosperity for many, the power to develop entire regions, to foster the growth of human society."[2]

No one would deny that an involvement with capital would have its own dangers. But it surely should have been clear that the "asking permission" syndrome was even less

[2] Heijke, *op. cit.,* p. 59.

capable of promoting the gospel ideal within this form of life. As the religious congregations became increasingly caught up in the modern institution, the individual member without economic responsibility became a cog in the huge machine. A life of prayer and fellowship still supported the lives of these dedicated people, but their economic position was untenable.

The economic difficulties of many years have accumulated now and are weighing down present administrators. The kind of lively, new endeavor that might give a measure of hope to the whole congregation cannot be undertaken because of financial embarrassment. Severe criticism of sisterhoods for their lack of professionalism might better be directed against church thinking and church policy which were unwilling to pay for professional competence. But this is by no means a thing of the past. For the most part, sisters are still paid subsistence wages in a world where training and schooling do not come free. The congregations have to get their actual operating expenses somewhere, and because they are not being paid for what they deliver, they are forced into schemes and business operations of doubtful character. Occasionally, one of these operations goes awry and becomes a public scandal; but that is not the worst part of them. The real tragedy is that the whole way of existence creates an image of dishonesty in the mind of the public. The tax exempt status of the orders will only lead to more hard feelings among people and more troubles with the government.

Religious congregations are struggling heroically to prepare their people for the specialized tasks that now need doing. Unfortunately, they have added to their own problems by maintaining an elaborate system of "houses of formation." It appears that if theology or psychology does not bring down the system, then financial considerations will. Religious congregations are currently providing free undergraduate education not only to their own people but to many other people who do not stay with the group. There would be nothing wrong with such a service except that the orders have little enough money to do the work they are organized for without taking on this additional burden.

We do not have to argue that novitiates, juniorates and scholasticates are a theological remnant of the Middle Ages. It is enough to say that financially they have become nightmares. It is ironic that young religious today are demanding that the order give up its institutions for the sake of a corporate poverty. The orders should indeed give up most of this tax exempt property, not because it makes them too rich but because it is a financial liability. The money poured into novitiates and motherhouses could be well used to support the people and the work of the order. If there is any hope for the survival of religious life, it would seem to lie in attracting people who are a little older. They would have the educational training, economic responsibleness and theological preparation that would enable them to enter quickly into the life. Religious congregations moved from the elementary school to the high school graduate as the chief sources of their new membership. They have been less successful in moving to the college graduate, though that is the way that American society has been going. It may be that they cannot survive with the invitation to the college graduate, but they will never find out unless they let go of the closed system that still exists.

The answer to the economic pressure is not that the pastor or diocese should raise sisters' salaries another ten dollars a month. That kind of move is never going to be a long term solution to the problem. In addition, chanceries apparently do not have much ready cash either. To pay people the kind of salary they ought to receive is in fact impossible for church administrators. Yet surely there are alternatives in twentieth-century America. What the religious congregations have going for them is that they exist. They have dedicated personnel waiting to tackle the problems; they can provide task forces that far surpass what other civil or church agencies can muster. To let all of this die simply because of inadequate financing would be a tragedy.

There are two directions in which religious congregations must move in order to be financially viable. First, church officials who wish the services of a celibate community are going to have to pay the market rate. That amount would usually be several times the current stipend. If the objection is made that all of the church institutions cannot do this, then the answer is that some of them must close. A five million dollar building is not a school, as has been amply proved in our society. An adequately prepared administration, faculty and student body is the essence of a school. If the faculty cannot be paid a living wage then the buildings have to be closed up or better still not be put up in the first place. In contemporary society, Edgar Friedenberg has noted, we have done well with buildings; it is the people who do not look so well. One would expect that of all of the groups in contemporary society, the church would be the most anxious to put its money into people rather than concrete.

The reception of a straightforward salary would change quite drastically the life of the religious congregation. A diocese or parish would no longer provide things like housing. The cost to someone would probably go up, but at least the fiscal responsibility would be clearer. At present, the huge living plants constructed for religious do not seem to be any great financial saving. Moreover, there are few greater obstacles to living with a sense of communality than these mausoleum-like structures. Economic responsibility must in any case become the concern of each individual and each community.

There is one hesitation we have in recommending that church institutions close unless they can compete in salaries. If economics were the only consideration and if there were no centralized planning, then very likely the most needed institutions would be the first to go. What must not be lost sight of in the complications of financing is that the church is the church of the poor, that is, the church is the group of people who serve the needs of their suffering brethren. The many institutions that the Catholic church has in the midst of the urban poor are not generally the ones that need closing. They are the ones that need more of the support of the *church*, that is, the people who include middle class and upper class. It is said, of course, that if church leaders started closing suburban institutions and shifted the resources to the central city, then the church would cease getting revenue to do the work. It can be said in answer that this line of thought shows a lack of trust in the Holy Spirit and an underestimation of serious, educated, responsible Catholics. However, if suburbanites do protest and do cease giving money, the only conclusion to be drawn is the need for preaching the gospel

and for reaching the adults with high-level religious in-
struction.

When one speaks of "priorities," it should not be
thought that there is a choice of one which excludes the
other. Nor is it a matter of saying that the middle class
suburbanite should become a second class citizen of the
church. The tasks with rich and poor are related and com-
plementary. The church is not about to abandon the
middle class, the whites, the suburbanites. It is a question
of doing a different *kind* of thing with them. The suburban
Catholic school may be a good school by American stand-
ards and yet may not be serving the real needs of the
church. It may be draining off money and manpower that
the church needs elsewhere. What is needed in most
suburban parishes is a more effective, efficient and eco-
nomical way to reach the family than by going through
children in a school.

There is no denying that such institutional changes require great leadership. That is why we have stressed in
earlier chapters that doing away with "superiors" is not
equivalent to eliminating leadership. One marvelous thing
that the Catholic church still has in its favor is the possibility of centralized financing, planning and leadership.
In contrast to the tangle of city, state and federal agencies,
the Catholic church has a regional unit with the capacity
to redeploy resources. The question for the church official
is whether in fact the church does exist in his diocese and
can be inspired by leadership that points out the church's
mission. Should the revenue of the church fall off drastically in such an attempt and should large numbers even
leave church membership, it would not necessarily be a
calamity. It would simply force to the front the question

of ecclesiology sketched out in chapter two. The church, it must be realized, is never going to solve the economic problems of the poor with her own institutions. She is supposed to provide in living testimony a concern which will bring out human resources to deal with the human problems.

This leads into the second major change that we maintain is necessary to make the religious congregation economically sound. There is no reason why the celibate teams should draw their salaries mainly from the church. There is much money available in government and private agencies. Some of it goes unused because there is no trained personnel to use it. If the church were to take seriously a commitment to the ghetto, it is difficult to see who else would be available for the job except sisterhoods and brotherhoods. Many of these people are already there, usually running church sponsored schools. This work, we have said, may be a very valuable contribution to the central city. At the same time, Catholic groups must continue to ask themselves whether in hidden ways the Catholic school may not be dysfunctional. The concern of the Catholic must be the education of the entire human community. In some places, public education may be very bad and the Catholic school may be rendering a service to the community. Nevertheless, the Catholic school will be socially responsible only if it acts as a prod to the public conscience and if it does not distract from the bigger problem the attention of a large segment of the community.

It is not our concern here to try to decide on the actual situation of individual cities. As far as religious are concerned, however, the need is clear for getting into non-church attempts to deal with these urban problems. The advantage of the celibate teams is that they do not have to decide on policies to deal with the whole issue before they begin to act. Part of a team might teach in a public school, while others might be in a catechetical center, and someone else may be in various jobs which pay little. The mobility and flexibility of such a team could be quite extraordinary. Backed by the larger federation of communities, members could risk unpopular stands and partial or temporary loss of salary. The team would not have great financial assets, but then there is no reason why they would need them. They would have sufficient money to give the community some small leeway in supporting itself and helping others.

Many people will probably feel that these proposals mean the dismantling of religious life. The radicalness of the change cannot be denied. Yet some bit of this is already happening and the future seems to lie somewhere in this direction. We suggest that the radical change be clearly asserted instead of trying to pretend that the old cloth is getting new patches. Unless the clarification is made soon, the religious congregation is going to get into a very ambiguous position, particularly with reference to tax laws. There will also be mounting problems among individuals who now have access to money but are being kept economically irresponsible.

As we said in the first chapter, the great sin in our world is insincerity. The sincerity of religious congregations is not wholly trusted by either Catholics or non-Catholics. This comes to a head in any discussion on the poverty of religious which is sometimes a matter of scandal, often a subject of ridicule. The problem is not as it so frequently was with the monasteries in the Middle Ages, namely, that the orders became very rich. In many ways the congregations today cannot deal with the poverty (of others) because they themselves are too poor.

The church must not lose sight of the fact that there are other evils besides poverty. Nevertheless, poverty is a great evil that must be dealt with. By supporting teams of people in the ghetto, the church can manifest something other than a "dole approach" to the problem of poverty. The poor in this country need programs by which they can help themselves, but this requires people living on the scene. The Catholic church already has thousands of people working there. A large number of them are being run into the ground and being given little encouragement. Church officials and religious superiors do not seem to realize the precious resource they have in the lives of dedicated people. These people cannot be worked seven days a week with inadequate facilities, little privacy and no change of atmosphere. It is time to rid these communities of the medieval concept of poverty and let them be. These communities already embody the gospel spirit; they could use financial help in carrying it out. "Sharing in the miseries of the world is first of all sharing in the world's struggle against its misery. More than ever before, we are confronted with the question of evangelical poverty in the light of the two-thirds of mankind who live in abysmal wretchedness."[3]

[3] Roger Schutz as quoted in *ibid.*, p. 65.

11. The Senior Religious

Religious congregations today are changing institutions. The accent is on the adjective "changing." As younger people become part of the institution, entering it from a technological world, they inevitably bring with them the thought patterns of that world, and exert a social pressure upon the older members that is difficult to accept. It is also difficult to resist. Those in the middle years of religious life are ordinarily not in the same position as the sister or brother who has served in a congregation fifty years and upward. This is primarily because the former are still actively engaged, have been making adjustments through their contacts outside the monastic setting, and are to a great extent highly educated. The fifty-plus group, on the other hand, have minimal outside contact. Unlike their counterparts in civilian society, they have lived a stable, established and regimented life during a period in world history characterized by unprecedented change. Since Vatican II, the plunge of the church into a social setting from which it had been largely aloof has shattered the foundations of all regimented types of existence. This social setting is characterized by personal freedom, individual responsibility and participatory democracy. To enter it, the aging religious must in many cases make a fifty-year adjustment to be brought up to date. In the present chapter, we shall seek to examine some of the positive and negative dynamisms operating in this situation before making a few

169

concrete suggestions for programs and planning. We shall be especially concerned with the religious who has retired from active service.

"Old age is many diverse things wrapped up in one phrase. It covers vigorous, healthy people as well as those so feeble that all their bodily needs must be cared for. Each person is his own time clock, some going much faster than others."[1] There are many stereotypes regarding the aged, and one does not have to know many older people before realizing how little they apply. In large measure, the quality of one's old age has been proven to be the direct result of all the years preceding it. There are lively, alert eighty-year-olds, and persons already atrophied at sixty-five. There are hikers and swimmers at seventy, and sad and sedentary recluses ten years younger. There are outgoing, unselfish and dynamic personalities whose physical appearance is in direct contradiction to their vitality. Nevertheless, the aged, whether in religious life or not, share certain characteristics. The first is their position in our society and our culture. The biological revolution that has resulted in the prolongation of life in America guarantees that our over sixty-five population will continue to increase. At the same time, our emphasis on youth, activity and physical prowess results in a feeling of uselessness on the part of many older citizens. It is to the credit of religious congregations that they are aware of this situation. As is true with older people generally—as against one misconception—older religious *want* to carry their full weight, though they often need more time to accomplish a particular task. In recognizing this, religious superiors

[1] Robert Havighurst and Ruth Albrecht, *Older People* (New York, 1953), p. 9.

see the need to plan with, rather than for, their older members.

Irving Rosow's comment that "problems of old age are of two general kinds: those that older people actually have and those that experts think they have"[2] is the beginning of one enlightened discussion where an author points out the oversimplification of many of the problems of the aged. He makes the careful distinction between sensitivity to material and social needs, the first concrete, the latter abstract. As Judith Tate commented some years ago, older sisters are often well-fed and well-medicined, but unnoticed as persons.[3] It is a situation summed up by one old man who noted, "People often talk to me, but they never really converse with me, and so I am alone." Congregations, in their insistence on community today, are facing this problem. In the introduction to this book, we stated our belief that the lives of those who have served faithfully over the years are the greatest testimony possible to the years they have given to the church; nonetheless, we are deeply aware that today they often experience profound loneliness. In saying this, we wish to emphasize our awareness that the social need is as great as the material need. What we would further assert at this point is the interrelationship of the two. As congregations solve the physical and financial problems of the aged, they will be moving toward a solution of their social problems as well.

Retirement looms as a major problem today for religious, just as it does for many of the aged. Kutner and his associates, in the sample of older people they studied, found that decline in morale went hand in hand with ex-

[2] *Social Integration of the Aged* (New York, 1967), p. 1.
[3] *Sisters for the World* (New York, 1966), p. 135.

clusion from activities providing status, achievement and recognition. The authors contended that "Not any activity but only activities that provide status, achievement and recognition can lift morale and those that are not basically satisfying needs do not contribute much to the individual's adjustment."[4] Several factors compound this situation for religious. 1) Having gone at a tremendous pace for fifty years and more, many have done nothing else but work and do not know how to fill an empty hour, not to speak of completely free time. From being full-fledged members of a community, facing hundreds of students daily, many find themselves forced to make an abrupt transition from thoroughly professional to thoroughly non-professional activity. 2) Leisure time for many has been equated with the daily hour labeled "recreation." Suddenly, the entire day has this quality of recreation. The unnerving aspect of this is that it must often be spent alone. Furthermore, recreation for many has been a time in the past *not* devoted to activities promoting status, achievement and recognition. 3) Perhaps the most serious factor for the retired religious lies in his lack of preparation for retirement. Unlike the professions, industry and business organizations, retirement has never formed a part of the normal religious's life span. Most brothers and sisters count it an honor to die while still active. A realistic assessment of the situation now indicates that retirement programs must be carefully planned and initiated long before the actual retirement date. Research shows, too, that the most successful retirees are those who have planned for and looked forward to this period of their lives as the natural outcome of the busy

[4] B. Kutner, D. Fanshel, Alice M. Togo and T. S. Langner, *Five Hundred Over Sixty* (New York, 1956), p. 104.

middle years. As congregations continue to develop and expand such programs, the question will become less critical. Nevertheless, at this time, there is required much sensitivity and genuine patience during the painful adjustment of older brothers and sisters.

As these older religious listen to daily discussions of involvement, concern for the world and relevance, it is understandable that they should question their place in the entire institution. The fear of being helpless, alone and unwanted that characterizes so many in the "golden years"[5] touches them too. Obviously, the question of income and the financing of medical care are serious ones in this context. What was said above with regard to poverty (chapter ten) is especially pertinent here. Part of the professional salaries earned by active members of celibate teams will surely go to the maintenance of aged members no longer in service. It is an accepted and unquestioningly held tenet of many younger religious today that all their talk of concern, involvement and service is the sterile mouthing of words if such concern does not begin with the older members of their congregations who have in fact brought them to where they now are. These younger members are often the most radical in other areas. Yet they are persons who hesitate to condemn the past, realizing that it is the past that has given birth to the present and that it is because old men have dared to see visions that young men are beginning to realize dreams.

Another factor in the question of the aged is that although problems of a lack of direction, lack of self-understanding, and lack of purpose for the inner self do not

[5] See Michael Harrington, Chapter 6, "The Golden Years," in *The Other America* (New York, 1963).

belong exclusively to the aged, they are magnified in their lives. This is undoubtedly due to reflections on the meaning of life and the inevitability of death brought on by the questions of time and the future. Psychiatrists have pointed out that at some time in the middle years, most people cease measuring their age by its distance from birth and begin measuring it by its distance from death. To hear constantly that this is a future-oriented world, and yet to grow daily more aware that one's future is shrinking can be a frustrating experience. The word "fulfillment" rises naturally to the lips of the young, but the concept is rooted in the bones of the old. This is the time of their lives when they must come face to face with several serious realities: an acceptance that their lives have been what they have been; an understanding that the end is approaching; and an uncertainty with regard to life after death. It is here that psychological, theological and social contributions can be of service.

In the field of psychology, the Kansas City studies of adult life have been among the most serious projects yet undertaken in this country relative to the process of aging. Flowing from these studies, one of the major theories to be proposed has been that of disengagement. Briefly stated, it is the "inevitable process in which many of the relationships between a person and other members of society are severed and those remaining are altered in quality."[6] Such altered relationships, analogous to those of aging parents who shift from control to equality to dependence on adult children, take place in the lives of active religious who must sometimes make painful transitions from roles

[6] Elaine Cumming and William Henry, *Growing Old: The Process of Disengagement* (New York, 1961), p. 211.

with extraordinary power to those with none. The problem is exacerbated where religious are identified completely with a role over a long period of time. Unlike the married person who may simultaneously be teacher, parent, friend, spouse and committee chairman, a religious may move, for example, from the one role of superior (which often unfortunately excludes the role of sister or brother) to that of subject. The difficulty arises when the shift in roles is accompanied by a swift and progressive deterioration in physical and mental powers, and an absence of cultivated interests, tastes or hobbies. An even more tragic occurrence is the continuation in a role after the necessary powers to fulfill it have begun to fail, that is, a situation where social disengagement does not accompany physical disengagement.

For religious men, problems of disengagement may be even more serious than for sisters. Culturally, men relate themselves to society through instrumental tasks more than do women, and the status identity resulting from such a relation is correspondingly greater. When a man does not have purely sociable skills and must mediate relationships through instrumental activity, the loss of role— social disengagement—can be a major crisis.

Theologically, recent developments with regard to eschatology and to the theology of death could be invaluable in treating of the question of the aged. Although it is true that the aging religious, particularly the one who is mentally alert, must be able to maintain a genuine interest in the developing contemporary world, there is a corresponding obligation on the part of the congregation at large to make known the present positions on suffering and death. This is especially true today when these are so characterized by hope. Here seems to lie the natural place to balance the tendency toward a closed humanism with an emphasis on an open future. It is not romanticism but cold fact that our aged religious are the ones taking those last precarious steps that lead to new and unimagined life.

Socially, the question of the aged is a total responsibility. This is to say that it begins with the aged themselves, leads to the congregation of which they are members, and rests as well on the whole society. In the second part of this chapter, we should like to consider each of these as they relate to plans and programs for the older religious.

In most religious communities, taken up with problems of apostolate and involvement, there are very few psychological discussions which consider the dynamics of aging. The much emphasized stress on the importance of the person often seems non-existent after sixty-five. It is sometimes taken for granted, usually without substantiation, that decline in physical ability is accompanied somehow by decline in ego-structure and in learning ability. This is simply not true. The preservation of the integrity of the self in the aging person is precisely what insures the wholesomeness or unwholesomeness of the total personality, and this preservation is a duty for all concerned. There is ample evidence that learning may go on indefinitely. Julietta Arthur cites an instance in Los Angeles where "twenty-thousand people aged sixty-five to one-hundred-four enrolled in courses specially designed for senior citizens, sponsored by the Board of Education. These eager students were so enthusiastic that the school board had to operate a six-week summer session because they refused to take a vacation."[7] In the field of education or re-education (called in-service formation today) for the older religious, discussions with them of the psychological, social and cultural dynamics of aging, planned on a definite schedule, are in order. Such discussions, in addition to helping persons understand themselves, might also have the therapeutic value of aiding in the acquisition of positive motives, values and attitudes where these are lacking. For there is at this time a need to realize that the person's own attitudes toward age and its supposed handicaps may be an obstacle. Not for a moment can other members of a religious congregation relax their watchfulness for the negative, pre-defeated approach that can be so destructive for their older brothers or sisters.

The superior-subject relationship is another extremely powerful dynamism. Training in the past has been in the direction of total dependence, and increasing age in the societal setting of the religious life reinforces this dependence. Some consideration must be given to how one would put this dynamism to work. Perhaps the often heard statement of the older religious that "If the superior says to do it, I will" could be used to effect educational programs designed to benefit the older person. Sanctioned by authority figures, they would possibly be more easily accepted by the aging person. How this will operate in a nuclear community where authority is vested in the group remains to be seen, but there is no reason to fear unwished for results. Where the persuasion of one may not be effective, the urging of many may.

An educational program might arise in a consideration of the entire question of change. One can support the

[7] *You and Yours* (Philadelphia, 1960), p. 143.

premises that people resist changes that appear to threaten basic securities; they resist proposed changes they do not understand; they resist being forced to change.[8] If change can be introduced in such a way as to work with and overcome these conditions, the assimilation of older religious into newer life styles might be facilitated. One must develop such a strategy by examining the process of change itself, by carefully selecting and preparing the person who will be the change agent, and by working for an attitude that sees change as desirable. Such strategy must be based on a thorough knowledge and respect for the aged persons and a sincere willingness to listen to them. Here it would certainly be advantageous to have persons of their own age—non-threatening persons—take part in any programs to be initiated. In the business world, efficient programs of this nature are taken for granted; in religious life they are not, and professionalism in fields such as introducing change into organizational structures is only beginning to be recognized as desirable. To learn techniques from the "world" still poses difficulties; unlike younger religious, older people were trained against any kind of secular inroads to their lives. Hence a compounding of the difficulty of accepting such new notions as freedom of choice, team government and responsibility for decisions.

Literature discussing the aging indicates that in any tactics and procedures that are planned as part of their lives, operations of two kinds must take place simultaneously. There must be programs of the most general kind geared to attitudes, values and beliefs, theoretical in nature, allowing time for assimilation and discussion. There

[8] Edward H. Spicer (ed.), *Human Problems in Technological Change* (New York, 1952), p. 18.

must also be highly specific programs where the skills, talents and abilities not only of older people, but of the total congregation, are mobilized in working with the problem. One example of the latter is the retirement program of the School Sisters of St. Francis, Milwaukee, Wisconsin. During 1967, a committee on retirement in this congregation met to discuss and listen to speakers, to broaden their views about retirement and semi-retirement. Following this, they interviewed each of the older sisters of their provinces personally. In interviewing, they asked only such questions as: "If you were to stop the work you are doing now (teaching, nursing, office work, and so forth), what would you like to do? Would you prefer to stay in the province when you are retired or semi-retired? What hobbies do you have?" Although the sisters admit that many mistakes were made, from the area of semi-retirement came the response from many sisters that they would like to tutor or help in libraries. About thirty sisters subsequently took a basic course in library work, and in the school year 1967–1968, ten were actually doing this work.[9] One major difficulty that many congregations would experience here is that there are just not that many school libraries. Nevertheless, the principle is valid. A congregation must bring to bear its creative imagination in offering options to its oldest members. One such option might occur where voluntary teams from local nuclear units agree to conduct weekend workshops in houses of retirement, or at centers where retired religious might gather. Such workshops could take many forms: ceramics, painting, sculpture; film, TV, communications; poetry,

[9] Sister Mary Antonius, *Lafarge Program: School Sisters of St. Francis Committee on Retirement* (Chicago, 1967).

music, drama. Other teams, drawn from local houses, might contract to be responsible for one evening of entertainment each week, not only to provide amusement, but to provide a person-to-person contact with younger, more active members of the congregation. Another variation on this theme could be the offering of college courses on a regular weekly basis to senior religious, especially where congregations operate local colleges. The Smithsonian Institute in Washington, D.C., offers such courses on a scholarship basis to senior citizens; many universities have visiting scholar privileges. Religious congregations can do no less and may even do more. This is an area where inter-congregational cooperation must take place. Smaller congregations should be made to feel welcome on the premises and in the houses of larger congregations; the interchange of personnel and the presence of new faces would be a welcome gain. The multi-faculty, multi-congregational Marillac College in St. Louis is one model for such undertakings.

Since a person's happiness depends in part on what others think of how he lives and what he does, and since this is particularly true for the aged, those conducting programs for them must not be arbitrarily chosen. Persons with various skills are needed. First, there must be "bridges." These are sisters and brothers within the congregation who have a genuine affinity for the aged; young enough to understand the impatience of the young, old enough to have experienced the isolation of the old. These will be persons of whom the aged may ask questions without embarrassment and whose concern is so apparent it leaves no doubt. They are the ones who will be needed to help solve the inter-generational tensions with which all societies must deal. In this context, disengagement theory can be viewed as a phenomenon that may function to soften the rivalry between generations. "A society whose organization depends partly on the assumption that science yields the only sure knowledge must somehow train its young in competence and retire its old, at the same time avoiding wastefulness as well as rivalry. It is hard to keep the generations from stepping on one another's heels; the young are often ready for authority before the old wish to abandon it. Direct competition between the young and the old for powerful and instrumental roles would be highly disruptive, because it would cut across many important alignments."[10]

Secondly, there must be specialists in geriatrics. Where congregations are too small to train or hire such persons, inter-congregational or diocesan support must be solicited. These specialists, once trained, might undertake several needed operations in addition to direct work with the aged. They could serve as educational liaisons to the larger congregation in the latter's coming to understand specific problems of the aged: that old people are affected by the elements; that they need to be careful of overcrowding and high humidity in which germs survive; that they do not tolerate abrupt shifts in weather very well; that a few small comforts (for example, a night light) can bring reassurance; that art, music and poetry are not the province of youth alone. They could conduct courses in aging as information for the young and as preparation for the middle-aged. They might also take responsibility for contact with national retirees' associations, such as that for retired teachers, to come to an understanding of professionally

[10] Cumming and Henry, *op. cit.*, pp. 219–220.

administered programs and to broaden contact with the wider community. They might also establish contact with the United States Department of Health, Education and Welfare, especially through its periodical, *Aging,* in order to be kept informed of developments in the area.

State agencies, voluntary organizations and governmental units already have numerous programs in operation which can be brought to bear on the problems a congregation faces in guiding its aging members. The Senior Citizens Service Corps of New York City, for example, has in the past advised older New Yorkers that they still have a great deal to contribute to their community. They could "knit, crochet, sew, play games, read aloud, write letters, speak another language, sketch, paint or woodcarve, sing or play an instrument, offer escort service, or be otherwise helpful. There is an urgent need of such services in hospitals, clinics, orphanages, settlements and a host of other understaffed institutions designed to add to the well-being of others."[11]

From examination of such programs, administration of similar ones or joint operations with state and federal agencies might be undertaken by the Conferences of Major Superiors of Men and Women. It is imperative for such organizations as these to take the lead in advising congregations of the wide range of treatment and social services available today that control or seek to prevent the problems of aging. They could also serve as clearing houses for the gathering and dissemination of the continually growing body of research and literature on the aged alluded to in this chapter. Finally, they could serve as resource base for small-scale programs relative to the aging to be supple-

[11] Arthur, *op. cit.,* pp. 136–137.

mented by aid in resources and personnel by federal and local agencies. In all such operations, contact with the White House Conference on the Aging would prove invaluable. To effect the implementation of these suggestions, a committee or at least a coordinator of retirement programs should be trained and begin working as soon as possible in every congregation of brothers and sisters that does not have such personnel. Though a small beginning, it is action that is imperative. It is the kind of activity that should be initiated at once.

12. Social and Private Prayer

There are few subjects which are as difficult to write about as that of prayer. Yet some advertence must be given to the question of prayer within religious life. In many respects, this chapter simply draws together the various themes of the previous essays. In particular, we would like to pick up the concluding point in chapter four, namely, that there is a private sector which should be as private as possible and a public sphere which ought to be as open and expressive as it can be made. To say that there are two kinds of prayers in religious life, social and private, may seem to be saying the trite and obvious. Yet a good part of the church suffers under forms of prayer which fulfill neither the social nor the individual need of man for prayer. Religious houses have suffered worse than other places the disintegration of both forms of prayer.

What has usually been at the center of religious houses has been a series of "exercises" that have not been badly named. They may exercise a person, but they do little for his prayer life. They are neither a community expression of its life together nor do they allow one to rest in peace with his own thoughts before God. This lack of both privacy and community is an inevitable consequence of the general law presented in chapter four. To the extent that the church does not live with the spontaneity of the Spirit, then public things become private and private things are made public. This law is not so strange as it may first seem to be. The basic question is one of primacy of the freedom of spirit or conformity to system. When the latter is the case, all tendencies toward freedom must be eliminated. Thus on the one hand, the social unit is restrained by an insistence on individualistic rules and actions; on the other hand, the individual is kept from getting any strange ideas by keeping him under the watch of the group. The opposite of this arrangement would be a group in which life freely flows outward; if there were such a social existence, the individual would be encouraged to have a private life to bring to it.

The rigidly patterned system of "exercises" was the logical expression of a way of life that kept life directed to the running of the plant. One would not wish to speak too harshly of a discipline in which many people seemed to thrive. Moreover, Catholic groups today, such as religious orders, are perhaps overreacting in attempts to throw aside all external guides to community prayer. The fact remains that the supposed prayer life often consisted in long lists of sentimental atrocities. They were sometimes mercifully recited in a foreign language or else so fast that no one had to consider what he was saying. The religious life may have produced great men of prayer, but the result could hardly be attributable to this cause.

Things have changed a great deal and there is no sense in belaboring a dead issue. Nevertheless, though the outward picture is different today, one would suspect that attitudes have not changed much. The old system of regularities can no longer be enforced, but it is not evident that anything really new has grown up in its place. For example, the adoption of a shortened divine office by brotherhoods and sisterhoods seemed a welcome relief from the community prayer book. The recitation of psalms was an immeasurable improvement over the repetition of arbitrarily chosen prayers. Yet it would be difficult to find many religious to whom this office means much or who find it sustaining to their lives. It is less painful than the old prayers but recited with just about the same attention and the same meaningfulness. Part of the difficulty is the product being used. (The incredible doggerel of half-translated Latin hymns which people put up with is indicative of something.) Part of the problem is that the office was substituted for the old prayer book with little advertence to the fact that something else should have changed along with the book.

More serious still is the question of eucharistic celebration in religious houses. The most conspicuous thing about Mass in many religious houses today is the emptiness of the pews. It is not that nothing is being tried to improve the performance. All kinds of things are tried to make it more attractive, but with the strange result that the more up to date it is made, the more irrelevant people find it. No doubt there are places where there is one hundred per cent attendance at daily Mass, but this is even more frightening given the general attitude. In a vast number of places the Eucharist does not function as the center of the community. The least we can do is to stop pretending with a lot of rhetoric that it does, since this only frustrates people all the more.

In order to understand the problem of liturgical prayer in religious life, it is necessary to keep in mind the liturgical crisis affecting the whole Catholic church. The long years of liturgical reform came to a glorious conclusion, it was thought, with the official approval of the new liturgy early in the Council. But as we have several times pointed out, if one is going to leave a carefully defined system, one had better be ready for a quantum leap. To this day it does not seem to have come through to church leaders that translated prayers, inserted hymns and changed rituals leave *everyone* malcontent. A few years ago there was a clear cut battle between the liturgists who wanted change and the conservatives who wanted no change. More recently, the lines have not only become blurred; the roles often seem to have reversed. People who had steadfastly resisted any of the liturgy business now often sing the loudest, offer their petitions and hit all the proper responses. In contrast, the progressive who once diligently worked for all these things can now often be found outside the chapel or, if inside, standing mute with a pained look on his face.

It is, therefore, missing the point to think that the disagreement is between those who advocate change and those who do not. Not that everyone has become change-oriented. It is rather that those who do not like change have found the most powerful weapon against it: small change. If small changes are not only allowed but even legislated, then people who demand major changes are effectively stopped. Their disagreement with current changes proves that they are unimaginative, unappreciative or impatient. These more radical change-minded people protest against the present rate of change because they feel that these changes only cloud the decisive issues and create an illusion of progress.

This difference in theory of social change is obviously not peculiar to church or liturgy. The failure to reach any meeting point threatens to destroy the fabric of our society. Those who see changes taking place in rational and orderly ways are appalled by the suggestions of the radical. They cannot begin to deal with him because they cannot comprehend what the other man is saying. Those, on the other hand, who are calling for a revolution are often quite disdainful of the orderly minded guardians of society. The inherent difficulty of the radical movement is that it attracts the best and the worst, that is, those who see beyond rational answers and have the courage of their convictions but also those who are too lazy to do any homework and feel that acting is easier than thinking.

In the sphere of liturgical change, the same dynamisms are currently at work. In the last few years a revolutionary element has become evident in liturgical change. It is now known, even in the public press, that whatever may come from Rome or the local chancery, there are quite a number of groups that simply do whatever they think appropriate for liturgical celebrations. These people are not just a few cranks out on the periphery of the church; the groups include many people who are generally considered among the most responsible members of the church.

This development may be a good one; it seems in any case to be an inevitable one. But the responsible people in the church are also aware that this is a very dangerous movement which could lead to schism or chaos. The crucial question always in the background is the existence of stable and responsible communities of people. This is why it is quite irrelevant how few or how many changes there are. Attempts at liturgical change in parishes had the effect of revealing that the parish is not a local community. The failure to achieve anything very meaningful in the parish is not due to some error in programming the changes but rather to the existence of the parish as the ecclesiastical unit.

There may, therefore, be no solution at all on the parochial level. One would not wish simply to dismiss many great things going on in parishes. Nevertheless, the church is at an impasse because of the presumption that the best way to divide up Catholics is by where they live and that to gather a few hundred of them in a strange building is the best way to celebrate liturgy. If the church is ever going to find a new liturgy, it will have to be by finding the church where it is, where people live together, work together or recreate together.

Since community is the underlying problem of community prayer, one would expect that the religious house would be an ideal place to develop new liturgical forms. Yet the religious houses are to a large extent centers of stagnation. One can see more knicknacks there than in the parish church, but the one essential note of a community spontaneously expressing itself in prayer is seldom present. This is a rather frightening picture when one recalls that the liturgy is supposedly the peak expression of the community life shared outside the liturgy. Perhaps these "model communities" have a richer life than is indicated by their liturgies, but the liturgical situation does not bode well for religious life as a whole.

To bring about major reform of liturgy in religious houses seems to be a nearly impossible task. But neither for the existence of the religious congregation nor for the service to the larger church can the attempt be abandoned. Few of the root causes to the obstinacy are usually uncovered, but a few obvious things can be pointed to. There is in the first place an inherited tendency to follow to detail the prescriptions of the local chancery. In this instance the leadership has been so lacking that the liturgical movement is scattered in fragments. The responsibility of the religious communities to the church at present would seem to be to take up some of the reins of leadership. This would be done by carrying out the liturgy in any way that seems responsible to them. There comes a moment in dialogue for a long stretch of silence.

It is doubtful, however, that this is the main problem of liturgy in religious houses. One does not get the sense of a chafing at the bit of episcopal restrictions. It is closer to the point to note that the Mass used to be one of the string of "exercises" and has never quite escaped from there. The action and words are mechanically reproduced day by day. Just as the parochial structure is based upon a world cut up into little geographical units, so the religious life is constructed of little temporal units. The Mass fills its proper place (usually early morning) on the daily schedule. There is a deadening failure here to break out of a medieval pattern of life with its sequence into which life was fitted.

The question quite simply is one of rhythm. When person, community and freedom are primary, so that nature, system and determinism are subsidiary, then one must live according to rhythm and not programmed sequences. The rhythm must be discovered by each individual in the interaction of himself and the primary groups with whom he lives. There are obviously patterns of being born and dying, eating and sleeping, playing and working. Human nature is not infinitely malleable. Nevertheless, human beings are presently in the stage of exploring how far they can break from their submission to the naturally given structures of earthly existence.

By taking upon himself this task of creating his own personal mode of existence, man has undoubtedly put himself into a precarious position. He is not sure where the limits of malleability are. He is a creature born of earth who cannot rationalize away his animal heritage. In trying to improve upon creation, man has made mistakes and probably will make many more. The attempt itself, however, cannot be abandoned; it is part of the project of becoming human. Man's specificity resides in his capacity to break with the laws of nature and create a new kind of order. Any moral law of nature requires man not to be subservient to what is given to him, but only to form a more human order in which all things can be.

Contrary to what is often assumed, this modern framework does not edge out the liturgy. Rather, for the first time Christian liturgy can come fully into its own, as a celebration of freedom in a community of persons. All the natural elements that have in the past gotten the main attention remain a part of liturgy but only as residual to personhood. The liturgy as a peak expression of a community life makes full sense only when there are such communities discovering and helping to create their own rhythm of life. When the liturgy is executed daily at 7 A.M. or Sundays at 11 A.M., this pattern may correspond to the rhythm of some groups, but if so, it is only by accident. By the looks of most parishes, not many people in the modern world function on this rhythm. In parishes around the country, the Mass is said every morning in an almost empty church. What is most amazing is that it occurs to almost no one that this performance has lost all contact with people in twentieth-century America. One can grant that no one knows exactly where to move. But almost any imaginative approach to finding people where they are could hardly be any less successful.

One would expect the religious to be the exception to the general pattern. After all, they are intentionally and explicitly engaged in being a Christian community of free, adult persons. Unfortunately, they are not an exception at all. If anything is true, there is less advertence here to the rhythm that actually constitutes the life of the people. Very often sisters and brothers are simply forced into the parochial structure of worship. This structure is itself the problem that the religious community should be challenging. When the religious community has its own eucharistic service, the result is often not much better. The parochial mentality gets carried across the street. The problem will not be adequately dealt with until sisters and brothers can serve as priests to their own communities. The reliance upon an outside minister for the Eucharist is at best an unknown factor. For the present, religious communities add to their problems by maintaining daily Mass. They might give up this norm if for no other reason than that they would have a better chance of getting the kind of priestly service they want by arranging it when possible.

The deeper issue here is not that the community has not discovered its rhythm, but that the community has not discovered itself. There is no finding of the rhythm because there is no community to look for it. We have spoken previously of the presence of community everywhere but the need to guarantee conditions in order that a community be operative, experiential and supportive. As one would expect, the need for grouping people in small experiential networks becomes most evident in the liturgy. If a group had the kind of revelational-redemptive experience we spoke of, then the liturgy of that group would simply be the eucharistic recognition of this experience. On the other hand, nothing more reveals the incapacitation of the religious community than its helplessness in this liturgical area.

A community discovering and using the rhythm of its own life realistically presupposes a rather small number of people. The liturgy, it is true, is a social activity with its own formal structure. The structures are ones which by definition the individual must come forward to meet. Built into the liturgy is a formality which makes it never entirely satisfactory to the emotional reactions of the individual. For example, the communal tone of prayer may be one of great joy just when the individual is suffering some personal sorrow.

The demand upon the individual vis-à-vis community structure does not prove that large, impersonal operations are acceptable. Far from indicating that, this fact makes more obvious the need to have small communities in which each individual knows the real feelings of all the others. Otherwise, what can be the gentle calling forth of brother to brother can more often be the violent wrenching of heartless strangers or the dull uselessness of impersonal formalism. There are no doubt times when larger numbers can celebrate the liturgy, particularly if there is an urgent and specific task that unites them. However, the continuing sustenance of one's life must be built up from the celebration of life with those few who are his daily companions.

Where there do exist such Christian groups, then all

their community experiences become liturgy. This is not a pious sentiment nor an invalid extension of the word. The liturgy is where the church is at prayer. Such a group is the church and their life of care for each other is certainly prayer. The granting of official ministerial power to the father in his family or the brother and sister in their communities, would further stabilize these communities. It would give a whole new burst of life to the church universal.

When this point is made to church officials, they often point out that these communities should develop "para-liturgical" practices. But these groups do not need artificially contrived services, ineptly called para-liturgical. They already have plenty of liturgy in their lives; what they need is the Eucharist. Our age is one of great simplicity in prayer. Most people can live with very few formal prayer services. Most younger religious see no reason for attending Mass daily. Yet they would be the first to say that they cannot go on for long without the Eucharist. They look for a Eucharist that is truly *this* community's expression of its own life. Far from losing a love for the Mass they more than ever appreciate it. In their world view, however, when you deal with infinities, the quality of them outweighs the quantity of them.

There is another principle that has frequently recurred in this book that is operative here. We have stressed that a community can exist only as it looks beyond itself. There are moments for simply strengthening the bonds that bind the few members; nonetheless, what enlivens the group is the life that goes outward from them. This outgoing orientation is a key element to the liturgy. One finds, particularly in seminaries and novitiates, but perhaps in all religious houses, a closed-in feeling that develops from intramural productions of liturgy. The problem would be partly solved by breaking the group into smaller units, but that is not the heart of the issue. The celibate group needs on occasion to pray with those beyond that community. Talking about "the world" is not much of a substitute for being there; that is, mixing with other communities, both men and women, Catholic and non-Catholic. If there is any life in the celibate group, it will not be threatened by sometimes functioning as a corps group to another community.

The religious community, for its own survival and for the service of the larger community, should be a place of prayer and reflectiveness always open beyond itself. Some religious houses do and should make this their main apostolic function. All religious communities ought to provide an element of this *shalom* just in being what they are. Those orders which run "retreat houses" unfortunately do not usually operate by bringing outsiders into the life of the community. It is easy enough to run a retreat house; it is more difficult but far more important to be a community sharing a life with outsiders. Our previous chapters, particularly the one on secularity, do not lead to a call for the dissolution of such prayer centers but for strengthening them.

The contemporary world has a desperate need for communities of charity, prayer and peace in its midst. Because Christianity has not filled the gap, various other forms have developed. Sessions of group experience have taken over what the retreat might have been. The group training center is usually secular in character. For that very reason it may be closer to the Christian conception than are retreat or prayer centers sticky with pietism. A Christian celibate group, not through sophisticated techniques, but just in being itself, could make an invaluable contribution in this area. If the members would trust in the validity of their secular task, they could patiently wait for the few who might want to celebrate in an explicitly Christian way.

This kind of liturgical stance requires men who are self-possessed, disciplined, balanced human beings. Words such as "asceticism" and "meditation" do not awaken much enthusiasm these days, but there is certainly something here that the earlier tradition tried to capture. Perhaps longer contact with Eastern religions will force us to rediscover some of these roots. In reacting against individualistic forms of piety, it would be unfortunate if the individual were denied both the right and necessity of his own prayer life. We do not have a choice between social forms of prayer and a private sphere of meditation. A man who can engage in one can also see the value of the other. The liturgical movement has often suffered from people who thought that social expression implied incessant sound and movement.

We have called this chapter "Social and Private Prayer" rather than as might be expected "Communal and Personal Prayer." The latter combination is too easily turned into a cliché which covers over all strong contrasts. All prayer, insofar as it is human, is at once personal and communal. What needs affirmation today are the two poles that are in sharp contrasting complementarity: namely, the visible, physical expression of a community and at the same time the deep, inner reflectiveness of each person.

Every individual in the celibate team needs the time,

atmosphere and encouragement to develop such a prayer life. Putting a half hour mental prayer into a schedule is the easy way that has usually been taken to solve this problem. Much more than that is needed today. A good education, including strong scriptural-theological study, would normally be one of the prerequisites. Living conditions which need not be luxurious at all but must be humanly as attractive as possible are also a necessity. Ugly, impersonal conditions can be lived with, but there is no reason for them to be allowed here. There is also the great need for sufficient leisure and psychic relief to sustain the person's life. Some saints may have seen value in enduring numbness in mental prayer. Few young people today can see any point in someone kneeling in an exhausted heap at 6 A.M. after he has been working until well after midnight.

How an individual faces God in his innermost self is his own business. A Christian would usually do it in large part by meditating on the texts of scripture and the figure of Jesus Christ. This is the solid guarantee Christianity has that its mystical or contemplative attitude never leaves the historical bedrock. By rooting itself in historical moments, Christianity does not drift into an undifferentiated, all embracing deity or absolute. The liturgical reading in this respect ought to be a big help in providing scriptural reflection for the individual. Unfortunately, religious houses do not seem to be using any better than parishes the concept of a continuous, intelligent reading of scripture. More often than not, one gets offered the mumble of a chopped up pericope seldom followed by any kind of worthwhile homiletic comment.

We are a church that greatly needs prayer. Of all the

groups that need it, the celibate groups probably need it the most. It so happens, however, that within these groups the most violent reaction is taking place against the imposition of a prayer life. One can hope that out of this reaction there will come forth a new, invigorated, personally assimilated devotion to prayer. It will be a disastrous change if all sense of disciplined rhythm is lost. It will be a very healthy movement if it leads to the formation of the small group that decides for itself on the prayer rhythm of the community. If the group can come to any agreement on their prayer life, the pattern will eventually grow richer. For the moment, however, all the excess baggage must go. Until we drop the pretense of a prayer life which is nothing but a dead formality, we will never begin facing the problem. If we cannot immediately practice the presence of God, it is something in our day to recognize his absence.

Nowhere more than in prayer do human beings put up the pretense that things are getting along well when actually it is not so at all. They sometimes remark that they are having trouble reaching the ideal but they are quite sure of the ideal. People hold an ideal of prayer which they picked up in childhood or in a novitiate. They struggle vainly after the ideal, but so long as the ideal is there they feel some measure of security. Every once and a while a retreat gets them into the spirit of the novitiate again. Perhaps it is time to drop the ideal conceived in novitiate books and simply do what we can with the material that actually makes up our lives. An historical religion, whatever else it does, ought to look forward to where God comes to meet us in this disheveled, daily turn of events. At the same time, instead of obsessedly trying to perfect some Catholic system, we ought to go out to participation in the community prayer of other Christians (for example, Quakers) or non-Christians. By accepting our lives as they are and by gaining personal autonomy in our activity, we might find the way to combine passionate activity and patient contemplation.

Conclusion

We bring to a conclusion this set of essays with the same question that we began with: Should religious life survive? We have omitted many of the subjects usually dealt with in books on religious life. We think that we have touched on a sufficient number of critical points. These considerations do not give us the details of how to live the life, but they may clarify the question of whether the life has a chance in this world.

We think on the basis of our reflections that whether or not the life survives, it ought to be given the chance to try. We do not think that current attempts at "renewal" are generally attempting to set it free to try. If the radical changes in vows, authority, prayer and so forth, were carried through, they would at least reveal the possible value, purpose and authenticity of celibate teams in permanent association. Perhaps after all that, it would be found that the struggle is not worth it and that the church has found better ways to accomplish her mission. But just as with the Catholic school system, it would seem tragic, not to say inefficient, to close down the whole operation without seeing whether something might be done with it. At the moment we can only say of religious congregations what Lewis Mumford has said of the American city, namely, that we are optimistic about possibilities, pessimistic about probabilities.

The question must be posed as to whether reform of

many congregations is possible without splitting them into at least two parts. This is not a question of size; none of the congregations is too big, though some of them are too small. The issue is one of conflicting world views and life styles. It will be objected that unity must be preserved and that conflicts must be overcome. Yet the impression one gets is that present attempts at unity simply eliminate the most progressive elements who could contribute to a creative kind of renewal. In any social reform, premature unity is worse than conflict. It short circuits the natural human process of achieving integration by the union of equals. To give witness as a human model, the celibate community must strive for an ultimate consensus, but the transitional time of today is necessarily one of conflict. The conflict may find a resolution within existing structures, but possibly it may be necessary to drop the present organization and begin building again from personal experience.

The worst problem of the present is not that the progressive elements are being cut off by the hundreds and thousands, but that they are being squeezed out by the ones and twos. If there is going to be a split, this is not the fair way to do it. As it is now, the young girl who decides that it is not worth the struggle, leaves the convent, gets married and forgets the whole business. The religious life may be the poorer for the loss; the girl presumably re-establishes herself in another community, the family. The older woman in the convent who sincerely wishes to follow through on this life has few alternatives. What is happening now is that small groups of women disaffiliate themselves from the larger institution and try to develop a new community life. Without the backing of the larger federation, such groups will find it extremely difficult to locate their position in civil or church society.

The fairer thing to do might be to split many congregations into two parts. Eventually, there might be new unions and realignments; various kinds of federations might develop. In a short time there would probably be fewer congregations. A split of existing congregations is not the ideal, but it is a limit situation which may have to be faced.

A split into two parts cannot be recommended on the basis of age. This would not be valid in that chronological age is not what divides people. It cannot be denied that more young than old are progressive or change-oriented. But there are a great number of exceptions to this rule. In addition, it is not so much the young and the old but the middle bracket where there is great diversity and no divisions by age. One must assert against many of the young that the celibate communities will not cure their problems by cutting off the old. Presuming that some people will be permanent members, one must remind the young that they will get old themselves. It is an obvious truth, but one that the young sometimes overlook.

The split cannot be recommended either along the lines of liberals and conservatives. Undoubtedly, the division will be described that way by most people; this is unavoidable. However, almost no one can use the terms without a judgmental bias to one side. The terms are not easy to define and people are difficult to categorize. Furthermore, the confusion of meaning indicates that the terms are no longer very helpful in describing the spectrum today. Since liberalism has supposedly become accepted as the usual thing in America, the fiercest struggle today seems to be between the liberal and the radical, with the radical as likely to be called left as right. Strange similarities appear at what are supposedly the extremities of the conservative-liberal spectrum.

Any split of congregations would have to be on the basis of the work they do and how members see this as related to a community life. The uneasy alliance of monastic ideal and active worker is quite evident in many orders today. It should be pointed out that no group can be so active that it lacks all sense of the contemplative attitude which the monastery fostered. Nor can any group, even in the desert, lose sight of its active influence on the rest of mankind.

It may be possible, on the one hand, to give some of the work to individuals who prefer a more stable, structured way of life. Some tasks can no doubt fit this pattern. The monastery used to run schools and there may be some educational work today that would be better off in having this atmosphere. In addition, new forms of education seem to be on the horizon. Frankly, we are not very sanguine about the future of a congregation that tries to work on such a pattern. Nevertheless, we would be quite happy to see people have a try in preserving it if they wish. Who is to say that conserving the values of the past and leading a calm, steady life of prayer and work is all wrong?

There are, on the other hand, works being done by orders that require a fluid structure. Those people who prefer this active, mobile, flexible way of life should be given a chance, too. This kind of life has both the advantages and disadvantages of loose structures. Who is to say that this active, secular style is not a valid way to witness to the gospel? We are not saying that it is the better way; we are not positive it is even a viable way. We are insisting that this latter form of life is not really being given a chance at all in the present system. The latter group is considered the one that has to prove its right to existence.

The struggle in the church today is largely one of uniformity against pluralism. It is a puzzling match for the man who fights for pluralism. He cannot understand why he is violently opposed because he is not claiming to be right, only claiming the right to hold his own view. The pluralist does not grasp that the uniformist has staked his life on uniformity and his life is threatened not only by the arguments but by the existence of the pluralist. The man of pluralism does not see that by the very fact of not opposing his opponent he is in effect destroying him. The only way out of the dilemma is for the pluralist to admit quite frankly that he is a threat, that he is not asking for slight variations but for the destruction of uniformity. What is then required is a trustfulness of person (already aided by his admission) and a depth of understanding. He will then be able to engage in the detailed discussion of where the old truths go. In this way he may invite the uniformist to join him in a life that will preserve the main values which the uniformist has protected under the aegis of uniformity.

Our position in these essays has been one of pluralism; it has been a plea to give a chance to new ways. This proposal is a dire threat to the existence of many people. We have no desire at all to hurt or to destroy, but that is not a choice for those of us who have something to say. The most irresponsible thing at this moment would be to keep silent. We can only ask the one who condemns these suggestions whether he does so because they are clearly wrong or because they offer a plurality of choice. If the latter is the case, we can only answer that we hope that the great values of past religious life will arise again in a multi-plicity of forms yet to be imagined. The time for action is now. The church no longer has the luxury of being able to wait for centuries or even decades to make such decisions. It is time for courageous leadership on the part of those who believe that it is worth trying to create the new out of the old.